HEIRS OF ABRAHAM

The Future of Muslim,
Jewish, and Christian Relations

Edited by
Bradford E. Hinze
and
Irfan A. Omar

WIPF & STOCK · Eugene, Oregon

Wipf and Stock Publishers
199 W 8th Ave, Suite 3
Eugene, OR 97401

Heirs of Abraham
The Future of Muslim, Jewish, and Christian Relations
By Hinze, Bradford E. and Omar, Irfan A.
Copyright©2005 Orbis Books
ISBN 13: 978-1-62032-760-9
Publication date 12/1/2012
Previously published by Orbis Books, 2005

Contents

PREFACE   v

1. Jewish, Christian, Muslim Trialogue: An Introductory Survey
   BRADFORD E. HINZE   1

2. A Problem with Monotheism: Judaism, Christianity, and Islam in Dialogue and Dissent
   REUVEN FIRESTONE   20
   Responses
   MICHAEL L. FITZGERALD   42
   MAHMOUD M. AYOUB   46
   Reply
   REUVEN FIRESTONE   50

3. Relations among the Abrahamic Religions: A Catholic Point of View
   MICHAEL L. FITZGERALD   55
   Responses
   REUVEN FIRESTONE   79
   MAHMOUD M. AYOUB   85
   Reply
   MICHAEL L. FITZGERALD   90

4. Abraham and His Children: A Muslim Perspective
  MAHMOUD M. AYOUB   94
  Responses
    MICHAEL L. FITZGERALD   112
    REUVEN FIRESTONE   116
  Reply
    MAHMOUD M. AYOUB   120

5. Submitting to the Will of God: Jews, Christians,
   and Muslims Learning from Each Other
   IRFAN A. OMAR   125

SELECTED BIBLIOGRAPHY   142
INTERNET RESOURCES ON INTERRELIGIOUS DIALOGUE   147
CONTRIBUTORS   149
INDEX   153

Preface

IN THE AFTERMATH of the terrorist attack of September 11, 2001, and the subsequent U.S.-led wars in Afghanistan and Iraq, and in light of the ongoing conflicts in the Middle East as well as in Africa, Asia, and Europe, increased attention has been given to how religious and cultural differences among Jews, Christians, and Muslims may have contributed to these violent situations. Some, with Harvard political theorist Samuel Huntington, believe that we are witnessing a new era defined in terms of the clash of civilizations.[1] This book seeks to offer an alternative to those who see only a future of ongoing contestation between members of these three faith traditions. Instead, we wish to advance mutual respect and appreciation, even friendship, and most importantly collaboration among the heirs of Abraham, building on the long history of such efforts and achievements. This approach does not deny the painful reality of interreligious conflict. Nor is it a substitute for the expression of lamentation and outrage at the human costs of these struggles. Rather, these essays are pursued in the interest of fostering deeper mutual understanding and appreciation of the three Abrahamic faiths, their traditions of beliefs, and their practices of prayer, worship, and service.

Our primary aim is to promote a three-way dialogue, a trialogue, among Jews, Christians, and Muslims. By fostering such a trialogue among religious leaders, scholars, students, and people of faith in local Jewish, Christian, and Muslim communities, we hope to promote the formation of bonds of respect and affection that can serve as a collective testimony to the goodness and glory of God and that can anticipate a future of collaboration in the work of social justice and peace. As the essays in this book attest, such a future of improved relations among Jews, Christians, and Muslims requires acknowledging our differences, wrestling with past patterns of prejudice and discord, and repenting of all that is unworthy of the God-centered life we collectively profess.

This volume began as a lecture series entitled "The Collaboration of Civilizations: The Future of Muslim, Jewish, and Christian Relations," which took place at Marquette University over a six-week period in the spring of 2004. Three of the most respected representatives of Catholic Christianity, Judaism, and Islam were invited to offer public lectures addressing the topic of the relation of the three Abrahamic traditions. We introduce them here in the order of the lecture series.

Archbishop Michael L. Fitzgerald is the president of the Pontifical Council for Interreligious Dialogue. Born in Walsall, United Kingdom, ordained a priest in the Society of Missionaries of Africa (White Fathers), he received his doctorate in theology from the Gregorian University in Rome and advanced degrees in Arabic from the School of Oriental and African Studies of London University. After teaching in Kampala, Uganda, and at the Pontifical Institute of Arabic and Islamic Studies in Rome, Fitzgerald served in the Sudan for two years. In 2002 he was named president of the Pontifical Council for Interreligious Dialogue. He has been actively involved in Catholic–Muslim dialogue and has also served as a consultant to the Commission of the Holy See for Religious Relations with Jews. He is the author (with R. Caspar) of *Signs of Dialogue: Christian Encounter with Muslims* (1992) and has published numerous articles.

Reuven Firestone is professor of medieval Judaism and Islam at Hebrew Union College-Jewish Institute of Religion in Los Angeles. Born in Santa Rosa, California, he was educated at Antioch College, Hebrew University in Jerusalem, and Hebrew Union College in New York. After his rabbinic ordination he received his doctoral degree in Arabic and Islamic studies from New York University. The recipient of numerous fellowships and awards, Firestone taught Hebrew literature and directed the Hebrew and Arabic language programs at Boston University before taking up his current position at Hebrew

Union College in Los Angeles. In addition to many articles, he has authored the following books: *Journeys in Holy Lands: The Evolution of the Abraham-Ishmael Legends in Islamic Exegesis* (1990); *Jihad: The Origin of Holy War in Islam* (1999); *Children of Abraham: An Introduction to Judaism for Muslims* (2001); and *The Resurrection of Holy War in Modern Judaism* (forthcoming). Firestone is the founding director of the Institute for the Study of Muslim–Jewish Interrelations (ISMJI) at Hebrew Union College in Los Angeles.

Mahmoud Ayoub is professor of Islamic studies at Temple University in Philadelphia. Originally from South Lebanon, he received his education at the American University in Beirut, the University of Pennsylvania, and Harvard University, where he earned his Ph.D. in the history of religions. Ayoub has received numerous fellowships and awards and has been in his current position at Temple University since 1988. He helped launch a graduate program in Christian–Muslim relations and comparative religion at the Centre for Christian–Muslim Studies, University of Balamand, Koura, Lebanon, and the joint Temple-Gajah Mahda Universities comparative religion program in Yogjakarta, Indonesia. Ayoub has authored many books in the area of Islam and interreligious dialogue, most notably, *Redemptive Suffering in Islam* (1978), the multivolume work *The Qur'an and Its Interpreters* (1984), *The Crisis of Muslim History: Religion and Politics in Early Islam* (2004), and *Islam: Introducing Faith and History* (2004), as well as numerous essays.

The essays in this book are arranged in light of the historical sequence of the religious traditions they represent: Judaism, Christianity, Islam. In addition, the three authors have prepared written responses to the other two essays as well as a reply to the two responses, thereby creating a written form of trialogue. This book brings together the revised texts of their lectures and their written exchanges. The result is a trialogue among a Jew, a Christian, and a Muslim.

The first chapter, "Jewish, Christian, Muslim Trialogue: An Introductory Survey," by Bradford Hinze, provides the larger context for the written trialogue between Firestone, Fitzgerald, and Ayoub. This essay identifies some of the most important efforts at bilateral and trilateral conversations between representatives of the three traditions that have taken place over approximately the last forty years. Special attention is given to the specific recurring topics addressed in these collective efforts.

In "A Problem with Monotheism: Judaism, Christianity, and Islam in Dialogue and Dissent," Reuven Firestone searches, historically and phenomenologically, for the earliest roots of the contentious rivalry among the monotheistic traditions. He finds them in the shift from a belief in many gods to a belief in one God, which is evidenced in the Hebrew Scriptures and takes place over a period of time as ethnic and national rivalries escalate. The source of the problem with monotheism, he contends, is not the shift from polytheism to monotheism, but the ascendance of an *exclusive* form of monotheism, rather than an *inclusive* form, after the Maccabean revolt during the Hellenistic period of the Seleucid regime. Firestone speculates about this transition, which provided a prototype for the destructive dynamics among all three Abrahamic traditions. Here he experiments with Rodney Stark's theory of the emergence of new religious movements as a means to illuminate the two competing forms of monotheism, Rabbinic Judaism and Christianity, as they arose during the first century of the common era.

In "Relations among the Abrahamic Religions: A Catholic Point of View," Michael Fitzgerald provides an analysis of the official teachings of the Roman Catholic Church on Abraham, and on the church's relation to Judaism and to Islam, highlighting the important advances that have been made over the last forty years toward improved relations, while also acknowledging ongoing differences and tensions. He comments on the history of bilateral, trilateral, and multilateral interfaith relations. His essay closes with a reflection on Abraham as a model not only for the children of Abraham, but for all human beings, as one who obeys God in a polytheistic milieu, one who trusts in God and confidently perseveres in humility, and one who enjoys a friendship with God and has compassion toward all in the human family.

In "Abraham and His Children: A Muslim Perspective," Mahmoud Ayoub explores the commonalities and differences among Muslims, Jews, and Christians as these are revealed through their shared, yet contrasting interpretations of Abraham. All three traditions affirm the common paternity of Abraham, but the divine promise, the divine covenant, is according to each tradition not extended fully to all descendants of Abraham, but is limited to Jews, Christians, or Muslims to the exclusion of other tribes or nations. The characterization of Abraham's personality in the Hebrew Scriptures, moreover, contrasts with that in the Qur'an. While many of the episodes recounted are the same, the intent and details of the narratives differ. Abraham for Muslims is not only a prophet, but a model of one who rejects idolatry and submits to God. Ayoub closes by proposing that Abraham can serve as the focal point for interfaith dialogue among the children of Abraham, one that promotes a dialogue of life, of belief and doctrine, and of faith.

In "Submitting to the Will of God: Jews, Christians, and Muslims Learning from Each Other," Irfan Omar explores the pedagogical character of dialogue, as illustrated by the exchange between Firestone, Fitzgerald, and Ayoub. Growth in self-knowledge is the first feature in this learning process of interfaith dialogue, not only in terms of discovering and witnessing to the deeper truths of one's own identity in relation to the other, but also of discovering and confessing the betrayals of one's own tradition at the expense of the other. Recognizing and acknowledging the religious other is the second feature in interfaith pedagogy. The commitment to collaborate in promoting justice and peace provides the third culminating feature in this process of mutual interfaith learning. Omar's essay closes with a reflection on the call to activism for the sake of peace and justice in the three Abrahamic traditions.

The editors owe a special debt of gratitude to Michael Fitzgerald, Reuven Firestone, and Mahmoud Ayoub for accepting our invitation to address this topic and to engage in a written exchange with one another. Their generosity has made possible this collaborative effort.

This original lecture series was made possible by the generous financial support provided by the Edward D. Simmons Religious Commitment Fund and the Marquette University Excellence in Diversity Grant. We owe a special debt of thanks to Stephanie Russell, executive director of the Marquette University Office of Mission and Identity, and to Judith Longdin, director of the Office of Ecumenical and Interfaith Concerns for the Archdiocese of Milwaukee, for their advice and support. This particular project builds on many efforts being made by religious communities throughout the Milwaukee metropolitan area. These efforts offer a significant example of the kinds of interfaith work under way in communities in the United States and around the world. In particular we wish to express our gratitude to the local groups of Muslims, Jews, and Christians who cosponsored this lecture series: the Archdiocese of Milwaukee, the Islamic Society of Milwaukee, the Milwaukee Muslim Women's Coalition, the Milwaukee Jewish Council for Community Relations, the Milwaukee chapter of the American Jewish Council, the Interfaith Conference of Greater Milwaukee, and the Wisconsin Council of Churches.

Finally, we wish to extend a special word of thanks to Pamela Shellberg, doctoral student in biblical studies at Marquette University, for her editorial assistance on this project, and to Susan Perry, editor at Orbis Books, for her generous assistance on this project, and to the team of people working with her.

BRADFORD E. HINZE
IRFAN A. OMAR

NOTES

1. See the original essay by Samuel P. Huntington, "The Clash of Civilizations?" *Foreign Affairs* 72 (1993): 22-49, and *The Clash of Civilization and the Remaking of the World Order* (New York: Simon & Schuster, 1996). For an alternative political analysis, see Fred Halliday, *Islam & the Myth of Confrontation* (London/New York: I. B. Tauris, 1996).

1

Jewish, Christian, Muslim Trialogue

An Introductory Survey

BRADFORD E. HINZE

THREE-WAY DIALOGUES among Jews, Christians, and Muslims—trialogues as they have come to be known—have increased over the last forty years. These have often been public, formal trialogues among religious leaders, academics, and occasionally with representatives of different governments. During the same period of time, there has been a growing interest in fostering more informal kinds of conversations at local levels among members of synagogues, churches, and mosques in cities and regions around the world inhabited by the faithful of these three traditions. In the interest of advancing both formal and informal trialogues, and in an attempt to situate the written trialogue that takes place in this book, this essay identifies well-documented instances and the recurring topics that contribute to this recent history and ongoing efforts.

Before exploring specific trialogues among Jews, Christians, and Muslims, it is helpful to acknowledge the numerous bilateral dialogues among the three interlocutors.[1]

Bilateral Dialogues

Jewish–Christian dialogues developed dramatically and painfully in the second half of the twentieth century in response to the atrocities of the program of genocide of Jews advanced by Nazi Germany. In 1947, Jules Isaacs, the French Jewish survivor and author, with Paul Démann, a Catholic priest, convened a formal dialogue of Jews, Protestants, and Catholics in Seelisberg, Switzerland; together they issued a joint statement addressing the problems of Christian anti-Semitism. In Germany a group of Jews and Catholics known as the Freiburg Circle entered into ongoing discussions to collaborate against anti-Semitism as it impacted German social and political life. In 1965 the first two formal dialogues between Jews and Catholics took place, one in Philadelphia and the other in Chicago, as the bishops of the world prepared for the final session of Vatican Council II, at which they approved the Declaration on the Relation of the Church to Non-Christian Religions (*Nostra Aetate*), which affirmed the "common spiritual heritage" Jews and Christians share, and repudiated anti-Semitism, and more generally paved the way for ongoing interfaith dialogues.[2] The World Council of Churches (WCC) addressed Nazi atrocities against the Jews at its first international assembly in 1948 and began a formal process of dialogue between Jews and Christians in 1965.[3] The International Council of Christians and Jews was established in 1946 at a meeting held in Oxford, England, to promote networking and collaboration among thirty-eight national Jewish–Christian organizations around the world; it has actively sponsored Jewish–Christian dialogues in a variety of contexts.[4]

These efforts at Jewish–Christian dialogue have devoted considerable attention to the search for sources of anti-Semitism in the Christian portrayal of the role of Jews in the life and death of Jesus and his followers in the Christian Scriptures, liturgy, preaching, and catechetics, and the need to repent of acts and attitudes of anti-Semitism. Attention has also been given to common and diverging convictions about God's election of a chosen people and covenant, the role of promise and fulfillment in biblical genres, and the divine gift and human task of advancing righteousness, justice, and peace.

Muslim–Christian dialogues entered into a promising new phase at the end of the 1960s. The first formal Muslim–Christian dialogue sponsored by the World Council of Churches took place in March

1969 in Cartigny, Switzerland; it was followed by a series of regional dialogues during the 1970s in Lebanon, Ghana, and Hong Kong under the leadership of the newly formed commission of the WCC devoted to Dialogue with People of Living Faiths.[5] Following the heightened attention of Catholic bishops to the heritage of Muslims at Vatican II and the concomitant increased interest of Muslims in forming closer relations with Catholics, the Catholic Church initiated formal dialogue with Muslims beginning in 1970.[6] Regional dialogues with Muslims have been initiated by the Pontifical Council for Interreligious Dialogue (formerly the Secretariat for Non-Christian Religions) for North Africans, held in Italy in 1988; a second for West Africans in Nigeria in 1991; and a third in Southeast Asia in 1994. The Royal Academy for Islamic Civilization in Amman, Jordan, which is a subdivision of the Al Albait Foundation, has, in conjunction with Anglican, Roman Catholic, and Orthodox Christians, promoted numerous dialogues, beginning in 1989 through the 1990s.[7] The World Islamic Call Society, a Libyan-based organization, initiated a series of dialogues in conjunction with the Pontifical Council for Interreligious Dialogue (1989–1994). The Spanish Association of Muslim–Christian Friendship sponsored a dialogue with participants from Arab and European countries in 1974 and 1977 in Cordoba, Spain. Composed of approximately eighty Muslim and Christian scholars from North Africa and Europe, the "Groupe de Recherches Islamo-Chrétien" (GRIC) has met regularly since 1977 and published some of their findings.[8] The Centre d'Études et de Recherches Économiques et Sociales (CERES) at Tunis University, Tunisia, sponsored dialogues in Tunis in 1974 and in 1979. More recently the archbishop of Canterbury, previously George Carey and now Rowan Williams, and Prince El Hassan bin Talal of Jordan have sponsored dialogues.[9] Numerous regional meetings have taken place to promote better relations between Muslims and Christians after the terrorist attacks in the United States in 2001 and the war against Afghanistan and Iraq, and in response to situations of tension and violence fueled by interfaith, ethnic, tribal, and economic factors in Africa, Europe, and Asia.[10]

In dialogues between Muslims and Christians, recurring topics have included the shared belief in a God who reveals amidst diverging convictions about revelation, sacred scriptures, and the interpretation of scripture. Attention has frequently been given to different beliefs about Jesus and Muhammad, prophecy and prophets, and the venerable role of Mary. A wide range of issues has been treated surrounding the fundamental requirements of belief: obedience and the repudiation of idolatry, mission and *da'wah*, faith and justice, and holiness. Ethical issues have been common topics: the role of religion in democracy and nation building; the comparison of Crusade, just war, and *jihad* traditions; the ethical challenges posed by Christian Crusades and Muslim acts of terrorism; and collaboration in the promotion of peace—as well as issues of marriage, family, the roles of men and women, law, economics, education, science and technology, and the challenges posed by secularism.

Over the last two decades *Jewish–Muslim dialogues* in academic and educational contexts, as well as at synagogues and mosques, have begun in earnest. Over the last fifty years Jewish–Muslim relations in the United States, the Middle East, and Europe have ebbed and flowed, reflecting the ongoing history of Israel and Palestine and in relation to the larger context of the relations between Arab and Western nations. Since the declaration of the state of Israel in 1948 and the migration of many Palestinians at that time, there have been ongoing tensions, wars, and acts of violence between Israelis and Palestinians and between Israelis and neighboring Arab nations. As a result, there have been countless efforts to promote political dialogues to address grievances about the right to land, statehood, and acts of violence in the interest of reaching a negotiated Middle East settlement (in 1979, and throughout the 1990s into the new millennium).[11] Jewish–Muslim relations remained strained by the ongoing violence in Israel by Palestinian Intifada and Israeli military aggression against Palestinians. The hope for relieving hostilities between Muslims and Jews and for promoting wider bilateral dialogues has been further complicated and jeopardized by regional violence in the Gulf Wars in Iran and Iraq and, increasingly, by terrorist acts of Muslim extremists around the world against the United States and Western political and economic interests, and the resulting action of the U.S. government. Yet, for every attempt to promote political dialogues, and for the many acts of violence, there have been innumerable occasions, often invisible on the stage of the world's geopolitical drama, when courageous attempts of individuals and even groups have created dialogue between Jews and Muslims in neighborhoods, workplaces, and markets.

The Maimonides Foundation began in the 1990s in London with the objective of promoting mutual understanding and cooperation of Jews and Muslims through cultural, academic, and education programs, inspired by the ideal of Jews and Muslims living together peacefully in the so-called golden age in Cordoba, Spain, at the time of Rabbi Moses ben Maimon (Maimonides, 1135–1204). The American Jewish Committee, which since 1906 has promoted improved Jewish–Christian relations, established in 1997 the Harriet and Robert Heilbrunn Institute for International Interreligious Understanding to foster interreligious dialogue in seminaries, colleges, universities, and learned societies.[12] Especially since 2001, the Heilbrunn Institute, with Rabbi David Rosen as the international director of the Department of Interreligious Affairs since 2001 and Dr. David Elcott as the U.S. director of the Department of Interreligious Affairs since 2003, has become a leading institution laying the groundwork for improved Jewish–Muslim relations. The Institute for the Study of Jewish–Muslim Interrelations (ISJMI) is being established under the leadership of Reuven Firestone at Hebrew Union College-Jewish Institute of Religion in Los Angeles. The ISJMI aims through various ongoing scholarship programs, conferences, workshops, and publications to bring Jewish and Muslim scholars, religious leaders, and educators together to study each other's traditions of belief and practices and to address situations of conflict and prejudice in an effort to promote better relations and reconciliation. The American Sufi Muslim Association (ASMA), formed in 1997,[13] and the American Islamic Congress, established after September 11, 2001, have been exploring ways to open dialogue with Jews.[14]

Jews and Muslims continue to struggle with the topics of land, verbal and physical aggression in the name of religion, and the prospects of collaboration in peace building. Grievances about stereotypical representations of Jews and Muslims in the rhetoric and practices of the respective programs of religious education and popular opinion have been frequently voiced. There is a need to articulate the convergence of beliefs about monotheism and the critique of the diverse forms and practices of idolatry in the contemporary world, and the larger set of related beliefs surrounding prophecy, righteousness, social justice, and peace.

What is distinctive about bilateral dialogues relative to trialogues? Bilateral dialogues, as this section has shown, have their own set of unique topics and concerns that result from the special histories of the two faith communities and traditions. Jews and Muslims converge on certain issues concerning their commitment to radical monotheism and their shared critical posture toward the Christian doctrine of the triune God, but they also struggle mightily over issues of land and statehood and the history of mutual prejudices, hostilities, and aggression. In contrast to Judaism, Christians and Muslims confess the importance of a central divinely delegated mediating figure in Jesus and Muhammad and assert the importance of witnessing to the message of the faith to nonbelievers (mission and *da'wah*), but they struggle with their contrasting interpretations of these figures and the threat of missionary appeals. In contrast to Islam, Jewish and Christian communities both revere the Hebrew Scriptures as canonical scriptures that testify to God's revelation, while the history of Christian anti-Semitism has been a particular obstacle.

An Overview of Recent Trialogues

What follows is a review of some major efforts to advance a three-way conversation among Jews, Christians, and Muslims over the last forty years. As will be evident, trialogues do not leave behind the issues raised by the bilateral exchanges—the shared convictions, aspirations, and contested issues. Rather, the concerns of bilateral exchanges are situated within a larger frame of reference and a larger set of relations, literally triangulated, which often complicates the effort to speak together and diminishes the areas for convergence. But with these added challenges, these efforts hold a greater prospect for enrichment and for establishing more peaceful and collaborative relations that can promote bonds of affection and the common good in local, regional, and international communities.

The Fraternité d'Abraham was founded in France in 1967 in response to the new initiatives toward Jews and Muslims at Vatican II. This group aims to reunite "those who . . . are attached to the spiritual, moral and cultural values stemming from Abraham's tradition and who are resolved to try sincerely to deepen mutual understanding as well as to protect and to promote together for all men, social justice and moral values, peace and freedom."[15] These aims are met by monthly conferences (between October and June) on a subject chosen annually and treated by Jewish, Christian, and Muslim speakers.

The Muslim–Jewish–Christian Conference (MJCC) has its origin in the first Interreligious Peace Colloquium (IRPC), initiated in 1973 by Rabbi Henry Siegman and Father Joseph Gremillion, the former director of the Vatican's Justice and Peace Commission, which brought together thirty-five participants representing the five world faiths—Hindus, Buddhists, Jews, Muslims, and Christians—in Bellagio, Italy, in May 1975 to discuss "The Food/Energy Crisis as a Challenge of Peace."[16] At this colloquium it became clear that the Muslim, Jewish, and Christian participants share much in common, but their history of conflicts presents obstacles to improved relations and collaboration.[17] As a result, the group was later renamed the Muslim–Jewish–Christian Conference. In 1976, the four sponsors of the Bellagio meeting, Matthew Rosenhaus, Cyrus Vance, Henry Siegman, and Joseph Gremillion, incorporated IRPC as an educational and religious organization, and William Ryan, S.J., became the executive secretary. Four interlocking areas of concern were identified by the group: (1) the changing world order as a challenge to the five world faiths; (2) the future of the Middle East—Can its three faiths work for healing after centuries of conflict? (3) religion's role in current struggles for human rights; and (4) religion as a divisive and/or cohesive force in today's interdependent world. Following this agenda, Gremillion and Ryan became the primary organizers of a second conference of the Interreligious Peace Colloquium, which convened eight Jews, seven Muslims, and fifteen Christians for a week in Lisbon, Portugal, in November 1977, and was devoted to the topic "The Changing World Order: Challenge to Our Faiths."[18] Professor Isma'il al-Faruqi from Temple University, who was at the time the president of the Association of Muslim Social Scientists, became significantly involved in IRPC and MJCC, played a major role in this second meeting, and ushered in a new level of involvement by Muslims. Both the 1975 and the 1977 conferences had three basic parts with papers presented and discussions: the first part was devoted to the social-economic, political, and cultural components relevant to the topic; the second part examined the role of religion and faith relative to the political and social issues; and the third part concerned strategic planning and public policy.[19]

The Islamic Studies Group of the American Academy of Religion, founded by Isma'il al-Faruqi, with the assistance of the Interreligious Peace Colloquium (Muslim–Jewish–Christian Conference), organized a special trialogue held in conjunction with the 1979 annual meeting of the American Academy of Religion. Cardinal Sergio Pignedoli, the president of the Secretariat for Non-Christians (renamed the Pontifical Council for Interreligious Dialogue in 1988), began this gathering with his keynote lecture, "The Catholic Church and the Jewish and Muslim Faiths: Trialogue of the Three Abrahamic Faiths." This was followed by presentations by representatives of the three traditions. The topics were: (1) the other faiths, that is, how one of the Abrahamic faith traditions understands the other two traditions; (2) the national state and social order; and (3) the faith community as transnational actor for justice and peace.[20] It should be noted that the second and third topics reflect the intersecting areas of concern delineated in 1976 by the four sponsors of the Interreligious Peace Colloquium.

During the 1980s, a number of noteworthy efforts at trilateral dialogues took place in the United States and Europe. In France, Jews, Christians, and Muslims met in 1982 for a three-day conference in Chantilly to discuss "Faith in Abraham," and in 1986 at a two-day meeting in Toulouse on the topic "The Search for God." During the Gulf War groups of Jews, Christians, and Muslims gathered together for prayer and study. The Al Albait Foundation Colloquia, a Muslim foundation, with the leadership of Crown Prince Hassan of Jordan, sponsored a series of dialogues in the United Kingdom: one was entitled "Muslims, Christians and Jews: Towards Increasing Dialogue in the Promotion of Common Values" (1984), and another was "Business Ethics" (1987). The Konrad Adenauer Foundation sponsored an international conference held in Salamanca, Spain, in 1986 and a later conference entitled "Understanding the Other," which examined stereotypes and began to explore scriptural traditions, took place in Bonn, Germany, with the cosponsorship of the International Council of Christians and Jews.[21]

In the United States an effort called the Trialogue of the Abrahamic Faiths began in 1978, with the sponsorship of the Kennedy Institute of Ethics at Georgetown University; it was directed at the time by Sargent Shriver and organized by Eugene Fisher and Leonard Swidler.[22] This group was composed of a total of twenty Jewish, Christian, and Muslim scholars, who met for three days twice a year between 1978 and 1984. The group met for the first time in September 1978 during the same period that the Camp David peace process brought together Muhammad Anwar al-Sadat, president of the Arab Republic of Egypt, Menachem Begin, prime minister of Israel, and Jimmy Carter, president of the United States. In the regular meetings that followed, attention was given to basic themes concerning how the traditions viewed each other religiously, distorted each other's tradition, and claimed the abrogation of alternative economies. Together they discussed their divergent approaches to commonly shared topics, such as revelation, scriptures, prophecy, salvation, and election and being chosen by God. The role of women and views of human sexuality were broached, and the contentious topics of conversion and mission confronted. This group paved the way for the establishment of the next international group.

The International Scholars' Annual Trialogue (ISAT) was initiated in 1989 by the *Journal of Ecumenical Studies* and the National Conference of Christians and Jews, under the leadership of Leonard Swidler of Temple University; it is composed of twenty-seven scholars, including nine from each tradition, with local participants invited and welcomed. The first annual conference of ISAT was held in April 1989 in Haverford, Pennsylvania. The second meeting was held in January 1990 in Atlanta, Georgia, on the topic "The Understanding of Revelation in the Three Traditions." The third topic was "The Dilemmas of Human Dignity and Tradition" (1991). The absolute as conceived by the three traditions—"The Chosen People—Promised Land, the Christ, the Qur'an"—was the topic discussed at the fourth meeting in January 1992 at Emory University in Atlanta, Georgia. The fifth meeting, held in 1993 in Graz, Austria, was devoted to the topic "How to Conceive and Implement the Good: A Self-Critical Reflection." In 1994, the sixth meeting was held in Jerusalem in the aftermath of the political situation in the Near East and was devoted to four topics: women, the relationship of religion and politics, visions of peace, and declaration of a global ethic.[23] In February 2000, ISAT convened in Jakarta, Indonesia, with about two dozen participants to discuss the topic "The Religions of Abraham Reflect on State and Democracy" at the request of former Indonesian president Abdurrahman Wahid. In other words, what is the role of the three religious traditions in the establishment of the nation state and the promotion of a culture of democratic dialogical participation?[24] In May 2002, ISAT met in Skopje, Macedonia, to address the interreligious conflicts among Muslims, Christians, and Jews that surfaced in the transition from Soviet control of the countries of Croatia, Slovenia, Bosnia, Serbia, and Kosovo, and the establishment of Macedonia. This trialogue concentrated on the promotion of interreligious dialogue among members of the three faith traditions as a means to promote peace and reconciliation and to negotiate conflict in the aftermath of the war in Bosnia and Herzegovina.[25]

During the 1990s a number of trialogues were organized in response to the repercussions from the Gulf War and the ongoing tensions in the Middle East. One such meeting was sponsored by the Life and Peace Institute of Uppsala, Sweden, and was held in Sigtuna, Sweden, in November 1990. The Japanese chapter of the World Conference on Religion and Peace convened a trilateral meeting in Tokyo and Kyoto, Japan, in November 1992. In May 1993, in Glion, Switzerland, a conference mainly for Middle East participants took place devoted to the topic "The Spiritual Significance of Jerusalem for Jews, Christians, and Muslims"; it was sponsored by the Holy See's Commission for Religious Relations with the Jews, the Pontifical Council for Interreligious Dialogue, the Office of Interreligious Relations of the World Council of Churches, and the General Secretariat of the Lutheran World Federation.[26]

In 1993, a year in which some positive movement was under way in the Israel–Palestinian peace process, The International Council of Christians and Jews (ICCJ) responded to an invitation by the Israel Interfaith Association and held a conference in Haifa, Israel, on the theme "Sharing the Blessing of Abraham in the Holy Land Today."[27] In recognition of the ongoing importance of the issues raised at the 1993 meeting, it was decided at the 1995 meeting of the executive council of the ICCJ to establish a new program, the Abrahamic Forum Council. The first conference brought together forty Jews, Christians, and Muslims from twelve countries in October 1999 in Berlin, Germany. The selected topic was "The Concept of Monotheism in the Abrahamic Traditions."[28] Papers were presented by scholars representing the three faith traditions, which were then discussed in small groups and in plenary sessions. The topic of the second conference was "Convivencia—Enhancing Identity through Encounter between Jews, Christians and Muslims"; it was held in Seville, Spain, in July 2000 and was attended by one hundred eighty participants from thirty-four countries, including Egypt, Israel, Jordan, and Lebanon. In addition to plenary sessions on the conference theme, there were workshops on eight different topics, some theological and others social and political.[29] In the summer of 2003 a conference was held in Utrecht, Netherlands, to commemorate the twentieth anniversary of the first ICCJ conference held in the Netherlands. With approximately one hundred people in attendance, the occasion was marked by lectures addressing the topic "Imagining the Other: Jews, Christians and Muslims in Modernity—Between Self-Determination and the Imagined Other."[30] Major presentations treated the gap between the ideal of universal humanity and reality and the debate surrounding orientalism and anti-Semitism. Some time was devoted to the three scriptural traditions. Lectures and workshops also addressed the concrete issues of migration, integration, and assimilation of Muslims and Jews in the Netherlands and Europe generally, as well as topics of the common good and law.

The ICCJ considered a proposal to formally reconstitute the group to include Muslims as members of their group. This idea was rejected. Subsequently and in response to this failed attempt, Three Faiths Forum was established in 1997 in the United Kingdom under the leadership of Sir Sigmund Sternberg, Sheikh Dr. M. A. Zaki Badawi, Reverend Marcus Braybrook, and Sidney L. Shipton. Their first formal gatherings took place in May and October of 2003.[31]

The American Sufi Muslim Association (ASMA), which began in New York in 1997 and is dedicated to promoting American Muslim identity and helping American Muslims build bridges with various sectors of the American public, launched in 2003 The Cordoba Initiative.[32] This program has many specific projects, including attention to the Shariah and fundamentalist interpretations of Muslim law, and various dialogue forums, one of which is called "The Jerusalem Dialogues," which will "convene a series of off-the-record meetings between influential American Muslim, Jewish and Christian leaders to build trust and seek common ground in approaches to peace that might offer just, secure and sustainable solutions to the Israeli/Palestinian conflict."

Conclusion

We have identified some of the most important formal trialogues of Jews, Christians, and Muslims in which a variety of issues have surfaced.[33] In closing, several basic topics can be delineated.

Starting a Difficult Conversation. Trialogues are pursued in the aftermath of acts of violence, when patterns of prejudice have led to verbal and physical discrimination and abuse, when loved ones have been hurt and killed, lives disfigured and destroyed, homelands desecrated and left behind. The pathway of trialogue appears as a way forward beyond the roadblocks and dead ends of interfaith estrangement. As a result, inevitably, Jews, Christians, and Muslims gather together in pain, grief-stricken, angry, yet desperately hoping to find another way, a better way of being in relation with one another. These are not the optimum conditions for fostering mutual respect and generosity of spirit. However, these realities require that one of the first steps on the way of trialogue is to find a way for participants to honor and name the grief, describe the source of anger, lament the loss. Out of this trialogue of brokenness, faith communities come to express their grievances about how the most deeply loved beliefs and practices of one's own people are misrepresented by the other's tradition, in their scriptures, in preaching, and schools. Out of the sharing of such grief, opportunities for repentance and reconciliation emerge, new vistas of mutual understanding open up, and new bonds of mutual respect and affection can occur.

Basic Beliefs and Practices. Trialogues provide the representatives of the three Abrahamic traditions with an occasion to set the record straight: to describe on their own behalf their most cherished faith convictions and practices. One faith conviction shared by Jews, Christians, and Muslims motivates all such efforts in trialogues: God has chosen to communicate with human beings, to reveal God's self through creation and through the prophets in order to invite God's people into relationship with God and with one another. Accordingly, trialogues frequently explore the topics of revelation and scripture and the converging and contrasting beliefs about the manner and the content of God's revelation. Special attention is often given to prophecy and the contrasting convictions about the role of Moses, Jesus, and Muhammad in mediating the revelation of God. The cherished belief that one particular people is chosen or elected by God has likewise been the subject of discussion and has been scrutinized for the ways it can lead to a kind of religious tribalism. Increasingly there are efforts to come to a deeper knowledge of the other communities through their scriptures and the interpretation of the scriptures, as well as through their practices of prayer, worship, and feast and fast days. By discussing these topics, trialogues provide a context to learn through mutual witness to one's own tradition the deepest convictions and most cherished loves of the children of Abraham.

Social and Moral Issues. Social and moral issues rank among the most frequent topics of trialogues. Sadly, it is often the brutal results of wars and their underlying causes that are discussed, but simultaneously efforts are made to sketch the social conditions required for peaceful and harmonious existence. Because the conflict in the Middle East factors so prominently in trialogues, issues of land and statehood relative to Israel and Palestine, and the coexistence of all three faith communities in Jerusalem, are frequent topics of discussion. Because of the correlative problems surrounding the rise of all forms of religious extremism and fundamentalism, associated with terrorism and state-sponsored policies and practices of aggression in various corners around the world, issues of human rights, democratic forms of governance, and a pluralistic approach to the common good are often discussed. Great concern is frequently voiced at trialogues about how the three Abrahamic traditions have been used to instigate and obfuscate economic, tribal, ethnic, and racial conflicts and injustices, and how these three faith traditions and faith communities can be drawn upon to unmask unjust practices and forms of idolatry that run contrary to the most basic tenets of all three traditions. Only rarely have there been discussions of family mores, the role of women, men, and children in the family, as these interconnect with sexual ethics, on the one hand, and economic and business ethics, on the other.

Collaboration. Since God's initiations of dialogue with human beings provide the basic impulses for the trialogue of the heirs of Abraham, and since God's intentions for a moral order in the world motivate every concern for being in right relation with God and with other people, it stands to reason that God's invitations and directives for people to cooperate with God's will for the cosmos provide the driving inspiration for collaboration among Jews, Christians, and Muslims. Ultimately, it is not enough to repent of the ways that one's faith tradition and community have borne false witness against the faith of another. Ultimately, it is not enough to make amends by creating an opening in oneself to learn from others about their faith. Ultimately, it is not even enough to form bonds of mutual respect and even affection among the children of Abraham. Ultimately, what is required is that the children of Abraham find ways to collaborate with God's work in the world of healing, reconciling, and bringing about justice and peace. This last step in the pathway of trialogue cannot be taken without following through on the former steps, sharing the pain of lament and the hard work of reeducation that call forth an expanded vision of God's agency in the world. But ultimately, the children of Abraham are called upon not only to be observers of God at work in the world, glorious indeed, but to be collaborators and friends together.

Notes

1. The attempts at multilateral interreligious dialogues of those outside of the Abrahamic traditions, such as Hindus, Buddhists, Sikhs, and traditional forms of indigenous traditions, will not be treated here. The World

Council of Churches organized a major experiment in multilateral interreligious dialogue that took place March 16–25, 1970, in the city of Ajaltoun, Lebanon, with thirty-eight participants: three Hindus, four Buddhists, four Muslims, and twenty-seven participants from various Christian denominations. What is noteworthy and lamentable was the absence of Jewish participation.

2. For background on Jewish–Catholic dialogue, see *In Our Time: The Flowering of Jewish–Catholic Dialogue*, ed. Eugene J. Fisher and Leon Klenicki (New York: Paulist Press, 1990).

3. The Committee on the Christian Approach to the Jews began in 1928 by the International Missionary Council and was incorporated into the World Council of Churches in 1961. See "The Christian Approach to the Jews," issued in Amsterdam in *The First Assembly of the World Council of Churches, Official Report* (New York: Harper, 1949), 160–64. For more information, see *Jewish–Christian Dialogue: Six Years of Christian Jewish Consultations* (Geneva: World Council of Churches, 1975).

4. See http://www.iccj.org/en/ (accessed August 10, 2004).

5. See *Meeting in Faith: Twenty Years of Christian–Muslim Conversations Sponsored by the World Council of Churches*, ed. Stuart E. Brown (Geneva: WCC, 1989); Jutta Sperber, *Christians and Muslims: The Dialogue Activities of the World Council of Churches and Their Theological Foundation* (Berlin: Walter de Gruyter, 2000).

6. For a general orientation to Muslim–Christian dialogue developed by the Pontifical Council for Interreligious Dialogue and a chronology of dialogues between 1969 and 1989, see *Guidelines for Dialogue between Christians and Muslims*, a new edition by Maurice Borrmans, trans. R. Marston Speight (Mahwah, N.J.: Paulist Press, 1990). Many formal Muslim–Christian dialogues are recorded in the journal *Islamochristiana*, which is published by the Pontifical Institute of Arabic and Islamic Studies in Rome.

7. The Pontifical Council for Interreligious Dialogue, *Recognize the Spiritual Bonds Which Unite Us: 16 Years of Christian–Muslim Dialogue* (Vatican City: Pontifical Council for Interreligious Dialogue, 1994); Michael L. Fitzgerald, "Christian Muslim Dialogue: A Survey of Recent Developments (10 April 2000)," Service of Documentation and Studies on Mission (SEDOS), http://www.sedos.org/english/fitzgerald.htm (accessed August 9, 2004).

8. Groupe de Recherches Islamo-Chrétien, *The Challenge of the Scriptures: The Bible and the Qur'an* (Maryknoll, N.Y.: Orbis Books, 1989) and *Foi*

et Justice: Un défi pour le christianisme et pour l'islam (Paris: Centurion, 1993).

9. *The Road Ahead: A Christian–Muslim Dialogue*, ed. Michael Ipgrave (London: Church Publishing House, 2002); *Scriptures in Dialogue: Christians and Muslims Studying the Bible and the Qur'an Together*, ed. Michael Ipgrave (London: Church Publishing House, 2004).

10. The Mid-Atlantic Dialogue of Catholics and Muslims, sponsored by the Islamic Society of North America, Plainfield, Indiana, and the United States Conference of Catholic Bishops (USCCB), Washington, D.C., issued a document entitled "Revelation: Christian and Muslim Perspectives" (December 2003). The West Coast Dialogue of Catholics and Muslims has issued "Friends and Not Adversaries: A Catholic-Muslim Spiritual Journey" (December 2003).

11. The most notable examples include the negotiations between Egyptian president Anwar Sadat and Israeli prime minister Menachem Begin in 1977, which culminated in the peace agreement signed with U.S. president Jimmy Carter in May 1979, the Norway discussions that resulted in the Oslo Accord between the PLO and the Israeli government in 1993, the Israeli–Palestinian peace negotiations in 1997, the peace accord in 1998 in Maryland, the Camp David agreement in 2000, and the "road map" for peace in 2003.

12. For the interreligious efforts of the American Jewish Committee, see http://www.ajc.org/Interreligious/HistoryHighlights.asp (accessed August 14, 2004).

13. See http://www.asmasociety.org/ (accessed August 17, 2004).

14. See http://www.aicongress.org/ (accessed August 17, 2004).

15. See http://www.fraternitedabraham.com/ (accessed August 3, 2004).

16. Joseph B. Gremillion, ed., *Food/Energy and the Major Faiths* (Maryknoll, N.Y.: Orbis Books, 1975).

17. For a list of common beliefs and specific conflicts, see ibid., 265–69.

18. Joseph Gremillion and William Ryan, eds., *World Faiths and the New World Order: A Muslim–Jewish–Christian Search Begins* (Washington, D.C.: Interreligious Peace Colloquium, 1978).

19. There is no record of ongoing activity of the Muslim–Jewish–Christian Conference or the Interreligious Peace Colloquium after the 1977 conference and the published proceedings in 1978, which was the inaugural year of the new Kennedy Institute's Jewish–Christian–Muslim Trialogue described below.

20. Ismail Raji al Faruqi, ed., *Trialogue of the Abrahamic Faiths* (Herndon, Va.: International Institute of Islamic Thought, 1986).

21. The meetings in France and Spain and those sponsored by the Al Albait Foundation held in the U.K. are mentioned in *Recognize the Spiritual Bonds*, 102-6.

22. For a brief history, see Eugene Fischer, "Kennedy Institute Jewish–Christian–Muslim Trialogue," *Journal of Ecumenical Studies* 19 (Winter 1982): 197-200.

23. See Leonard Swidler's history of the International Scholars' Annual Trialogue (ISAT) and the collection of essays from the gatherings that took place between 1989 and 1994 in *Theoria → Praxis: How Jews, Christians, and Muslims Can Together Move from Theory to Practice* (Leuven: Peeters, 1998); Swidler has augmented and updated his essay entitled "International Scholars Annual Trialogue (ISAT)" (2004, unpublished manuscript).

24. Papers from the ISAT meeting in Jakarta in 2000 were published in *Religion in Dialogue: From Theocracy to Democracy*, ed. Alan Race and Ingrid Shafer (Hants, U.K.: Ashgate, 2002).

25. The lectures from this conference were published in the *Journal of Ecumenical Studies* 39 (Winter/Spring 2002); they have also been published in book form in *Interreligious Dialogue: Toward Reconciliation in Macedonia and Bosnia*, ed. Paul Mojzes, Leonard Swidler, and Heinz-Gerhardt Justenhoven (Philadelphia: Ecumenical Press, 2003).

26. *Recognize the Spiritual Bonds*, 105-6; also see the joint statement from the Glion assembly in ibid., 105.

27. For details on this conference, see William W. Simpson and Ruth Weyl, *The Story of the International Council of Christians and Jews* [1946–1995] (Heppenheim, Germany: International Conference of Christians and Jews, Martin Buber House, n.d.), 99-103, 108-9.

28. See Proceedings from the First Conference of the ICCJ Abrahamic Forum Council, "The Concept of Monotheism in the Abrahamic Traditions," in *From the Martin Buber House: International Council of Christians and Jews* 28 (2000): 1-59.

29. See Proceedings from the Conference of the ICCJ Abrahamic Forum Council, "Convivencia—Enhancing Identity through Encounter between Jews, Christians and Muslims," in *From the Martin Buber House: International Council of Christians and Jews* 29 (2001): 1-233.

30. A brief report on the conference, "Imagining the Other: Jews, Christians and Muslims in Modernity—Between Self-Determination and the

Imagined Other," is available through the ICCJ, http://www.iccj.org/en/ (accessed August 20, 2004).

31. See http://www.threefaithsforum.org.uk (accessed August 18, 2004).

32. See http://www.asmasociety.org/ (accessed August 18, 2004).

33. Several efforts not included: (1) The Trialogue of Cultures was initiated in 1996 by the Herbert-Quandt-Stiftung in Germany, http://www.h-quandt-stiftung.de/ (accessed August 19, 2004). (2) The project "House of Abraham" sponsored by the World Conference of Religions for Peace began in July 2001, http://www.haus-abraham.de/ (accessed August 19, 2004). In addition, in the last few years, a number of universities have developed ongoing research centers, lecture series, and programs specializing in interfaith relations and especially in the relation of Jews, Christians, and Muslims. See, e.g., the Cambridge University Interfaith Programme started by the Faculty of Divinity.

2

A Problem with Monotheism

Judaism, Christianity, and Islam in Dialogue and Dissent

REUVEN FIRESTONE

ALL BELIEVERS IN ONE GOD—Jews, Christians, and Muslims—derive their entire spiritual existence from the same deity, however that deity is called. God is always at the center, and God is always worshiped as a loving and compassionate being. This refers, at the very least, to billions of believers among the three great families of religions we call Judaism, Christianity, and Islam. Monotheism began as a *unifying* system. Conceptually, it removed the universe and all its peoples from the fractious and uncertain rule of often bickering and limited deities and placed them under the mercy and grace of the One Great God.[1] Yet from the earliest annals of religious history, we observe monotheists arguing, fighting, and warring with one another through words and weapons about which understanding of the One Great God and the divine will is true—all others being false. What follows is an exploration of some historical and structural reasons for the long and violent history of conflict among monotheistic religions. I will attempt to examine the problem both historically and phenomenologically.

Origins

The story begins with the *emergence* of monotheism. It seems to have taken monotheism quite a while to emerge as a belief system in the long intellectual history of humanity. Scholars of the ancient Near East generally place its origins among the ancient Israelites, but there is still controversy over exactly when, where, and how monotheism arose. My purpose here is to explore the conceptual change from a multiplicity of Gods to one God,[2] a change that current biblical scholarship places in the exilic or postexilic periods (sixth century B.C.E. or later). While my approach certainly includes theological issues, I want to be clear at the outset that I am not interested, for the purposes of this study, in the theological problematic of "truth" in relation to the question of God.

There is wide agreement among biblical scholars and historians of religion that Israel did not suddenly come upon the notion of the One God. It was, rather, a process or development, and when I use these terms I am not referring to a Hegelian framework. The terms are intended to be value free and refer simply to change and focus. I treat the topic of monotheism also from the perspective of cultural history as I reflect on the emergence, inspiration, and influence of ideas across what we often refer to as boundaries between nations or peoples, languages, religions, and other articulations of human organization.

Actually, Israel may not have been the only community working on the issue of monotheism. There is that pesky Egyptian pharaoh Akhenaten, who, among his fascinating innovations in art, government, and religion, seems to reflect, at the very least, a kind of henotheism, in which only one God is worshiped while existence of other Gods is not denied. Some consider Akhenaten to have been a true monotheist.[3] A similar relation to the Gods and the cosmos is reflected in ancient Israel during what appears to be a slow and cumbersome movement toward belief in—and worship of—only One

Great God. Virtually throughout, the Hebrew Bible conveys the view that the God of Israel exists alongside other Gods. Even psalms associated with the temple cult assume the existence of deities in addition to the Israelite God, YHVH.[4]

While current scholarship is now chronicling a history of emerging Israelite monotheism, it is also uncovering expressions of monotheism that, like the religion of Akhenaten, did not survive the vicissitudes of history. Much later than the Egyptian experiment, during the period of emerging Christianity and Rabbinic Judaism of late antiquity, Greco-Romans held religious beliefs that, although generally labeled negatively by Christians as pagan or superstitious, were actually competing Hellenistic expressions of monotheism that were arising at the same time.[5] Although less well known, the Qur'an refers to pre-Islamic *hanifs*, those who turn their faces away from idolatry and to the One God.[6]

We have learned a great deal about the Israelite development from a near-contemporary Near Eastern religious system with many parallels to the religion of ancient Israel. Our knowledge comes from an archaeological site in Ugarit, in today's northwest Syria. This site has yielded a large library of religious poetry and narrative that has forced scholars to read many biblical texts differently than before its discovery.[7] In the religious system of Ugarit, the head or king of the pantheon was El, and his consort, the queen mother, Ashera. So too in the Judean cult, the writers of the Book of Kings knew that a Goddess named Asherah was worshiped also in Jerusalem, and she was closely associated with the queen mother, Ma'akah: "[King Asa] deposed Ma'akah, mother of King Asa from the rank of queen mother, because she had made an abominable thing for [the Goddess] Asherah" (2 Chr. 15:16).[8]

In another biblical memory of polytheism, Joshua directs a prayer to the common west Semitic deities *shemesh* and *yareach* in an old poetic fragment: "Stand still, O Sun (*shemesh*) at Giv'on, O Moon (*yareach*), in the Valley of Ayalon!" (Josh. 10:12), though the editor reconstructs the text to be an appeal to YHVH ("Joshua addressed the Lord and said in the presence of the Israelites . . ."). There are a great many more cases of monotheistically reworked polytheistic traditions in the Hebrew Bible that have been amply documented by biblical scholars.[9]

These are not cases of "straying after foreign Gods" (Deut. 11:16), an idiom that implies that the people of Israel saw the light when God redeemed them from Egyptian bondage, brought them through the Red Sea, and revealed to them the Torah. From the perspective of current biblical scholarship, it is clear that Israel did not suddenly "see the light." But neither did they stray after foreign Gods. What is denounced in Israel is actually faithful commitment to indigenous premonotheistic Israelite religious practices.[10] A partial menu of what was available can be seen in 2 Kings 23:4-15. This is the story of King Josiah's reforms, and it lists all the old practices by applauding Josiah's destruction of the means to engage in what appears to be the extremely popular and varied modes of polytheistic worship. He destroyed the objects made for Baʿal and Asherah and the "Host of heaven"; he suppressed the idolatrous priests who made offerings to Baʿal and the sun and moon and constellations throughout Judah; he tore down the cubicles of the male religious prostitutes within the temple itself, destroying many altars and shrines, including the Tofeth in *Gey Ben-Hinnom,* where people burned their sons or daughters to Molekh; he got rid of the horses dedicated to the sun and burned the chariots of the sun; he defiled shrines built for the Goddess Ashtoret and the God Chemosh on the Mount of the Destroyer; and he shattered the sacred pillars and posts.

Most of these were not foreign deities, the Gods of the hated "Canaanites," but were actually Gods *traditionally* worshiped by Israel. N. P. Lemche has shown that "Canaan" refers more to a geographical area than to a people, a land in which lived a variety of peoples that we know from biblical texts as Hittites, Girgashites, Amorites, Perizzites, Hivites, and so on, often lumped together in the Hebrew Bible (and Egyptian and Mesopotamian texts) as Canaanites.[11] The Israelites lived there too.

Israel, it now appears, emerged out of Canaan. To put it bluntly, Israelites *were* Canaanites, but they were one group of Canaanites who were experimenting with or were "growing" an innovative religious idea that would eventually result in monotheism. The Bible itself witnesses the bumpy road to monotheism. Why the arduous process, and why the near-universal change from polytheisms to monotheisms?

From Polytheisms to Monotheisms

Thomas Thompson has a compelling approach to the question. He takes exilic/postexilic biblical literature and places it within what Karl Jaspers refers to as the "Axial Age," a period from approximately 800 to 200 B.C.E. that marks a series of conceptual revolutions in human thinking from Greece to China.[12] Thompson locates the biblical Proverbs, Job, and Qohelet within an axial intellectual ferment that occurred also in the Aegean in the writings of such innovative thinkers as Plato and Sophocles, and less obviously in Mesopotamian cuneiform literature. The texts Thompson cites articulate a defining crisis created by the growing awareness that the old, past tradition appears to have seemed increasingly irrelevant.[13] The old polytheistic systems no longer spoke to the intellectual (and spiritual) needs of the time. The Greeks began rejecting the Gods and the cosmology of Homer and Hesiod for such as Plato's portrayal of the ideal philosopher. In the Near East, however,

> this intellectual crisis was resolved in the clear distinction between the reality of the spirit, the true abode of the divine, and the realities of the human world, including the Gods of human making, which are intrinsically partial and increasingly understood as fallacious. . . . Traditional understanding and religion were not so much false as human. Traditions needed not be rejected, only reinterpreted.[14]

By this time, the Achaemenid Persian Empire had united many national religions with their individual pantheons under the overarching rule of the Persian emperor, the king of kings, and the transcendent God of spirit, Ahura Mazda. If one traveled from the Persian heartland into Babylonia and on to Harran, Phoenicia, Philistia, or Egypt, one would pass from place to place but find the same Gods. They might have different names, but they occupy the same place on what one might call "the food chain" of divinity.

Thompson maintains that this unity of many political rulers under the one emperor, and the many ruler-Gods under the great God of Persia, evoked a kind of unified God theory that made names irrelevant. The history of empire forced "a world view that distinguishes relative perceptions that are contingent geographically and religiously from an assertion of ultimate reality that is beyond human expression, perception, and understanding."

There was a growing realization of the irrelevance of old systems in combination with changes in social-political structures within the empire. The structural changes in governance stimulated a reevaluation of the structures of the powers that run the cosmos. According to Thompson, the Greek intellectuals tended to reject the old system entirely for a new one that we call philosophy, but some Asian intellectuals redefined the role of the divine in the old tradition. Rather than a series of parallel Gods with different names—something like the parallel kings of small ethnic regions—there emerged the notion of a universal God, conceptually parallel to the emperor of the material world. This was an "inclusive monotheism" through which the God of Israel charged Cyrus, the king of Persia, to allow Judeans to return to Jerusalem in order to rebuild there the House of God (Ezra 1:1-3).[15] Thompson goes on to indicate how a pentateuchal editorial hand conflates the God of the exodus with that of Sinai and shows how YHVH is also Elohim, El Shadday, and the Gods of the patriarchs. The primary Gods of old that Israel knew became conceptually and structurally united in the One God, YHVH, who is also known by other names.

Thompson's conclusions correspond to my own work on divinely authorized or "holy" war in ancient Israel and the ancient Near East.[16] In this world, each nation or ethnic group had a variety of deities whom it worshiped, but each tended to single out one divine entity to which it felt a more personal relationship, and it was this God that cared especially for its people. All wars between nations in those days were divinely authorized—therefore, "holy"—because in all cases the national Gods of the various peoples engaged in one way or another in the fray along with their human subjects. To put it schematically, while humans were fighting down below, their Gods were bickering or actually fighting on high. Clear remnants of this can be found in the Hebrew Bible, such as when the God of the Hebrews defeats the divine powers of Egypt (Exod. 12:12): "For I will pass through the land of Egypt this night . . . and against all the gods of Egypt I will execute judgment."

An international worldview of polytheism that includes national Gods makes sense in a world in which basic ethnic independence with occasional and temporary conquest or subjugation was the norm, or at least a distinct possibility, in a basically level playing field. There was always the hope and the possibility that "our God" (or Gods) would help us beat "theirs" and thus provide greater material wealth and security. Most of the Near East, aside from Egypt, was basically a level playing field. Egypt was different, but Egypt's empirical interests and cultural influences seem to have had less of an impact on the Fertile Crescent than Assyria with its rise to empire.[17]

The rise and expansion of the Assyrian Empire permanently changed the face of the ancient Near East by imposing the phenomenon of super-king while defeating virtually all other rulers and their Gods. The empire God, Ashur, likewise became the "king of the Gods,"[18] as did the Babylonian Marduk after the defeat of Assyria.[19] The military unification of empire posed and then immediately answered the question of what was the value of the little Gods that could not defeat the great powers. Most local rulers continued to play the game in the hope of becoming rulers of a great empire like those controlling them.

So did Israel, or at least some of Israel. Isaiah 11 sees the Davidic heir as a just ruler, defeating the wicked and aiding the poor. God will gather up the Israelites and cause them to defeat their enemies

(Philistia, Edom, Moab, Ammon), after which the wolf will dwell with the lamb, the leopard lie with the kid. God will destroy Babylon (Isa. 12-13), Assyria (Isa. 14), and Moab (Isa. 15-16). In Isaiah 19, God will humble Egypt, and Israel will be partners with Egypt and Assyria in a kind of "G-3" (19:24-25). For Israel, it was only a dream, but some national peoples, like Babylonia and Persia, along with their Gods, succeeded, at least for a while. Most did not.

Like most peoples and their national deities, Israel tried to survive, but eventually was forced into defeat and exile. Much has been written about how Israel "prepared" intellectually for a final defeat through its Deuteronomistic reforms associated with King Josiah and others between the destruction of the northern kingdom and the defeat of the southern kingdom. Perhaps Israel's national religion was somewhat better prepared than the national religions of other conquered peoples who disappeared from history. In any case, Israel went into exile with its God, and some texts of the Hebrew Bible witness Israel's anger and desire for revenge.

Other texts, however, convey a different sentiment. Witnessing the grandeur of Babylon may have convinced Israel that it and its God would never defeat the Gods of Babylonia. Perhaps the overwhelming shock of the destruction of its national cultic center in Jerusalem forced a major intellectual and spiritual retooling among some thinkers. Some scholars trace a shift in conceptualization to the Persians, under whom the defeated Gods become equated with the empire God through the new title *Elohey Hashshamayim*—"the God(s) of the Heavens,"[20] and this term becomes a common one in the Hebrew Bible. Whatever the exact cause, the net result was, as witnessed by some biblical texts, an irenic repositioning of the God of Israel.

The ideal-typical expressions of this sentiment are the famous statements of Isaiah and Micah.

In the days to come, the Mount of the Lord's House shall stand firm above the mountains and tower above the hills; and all the nations shall gaze on it with joy. And the many peoples shall go and say, "Come, let us go up to the Mount of the Lord, to the House of the God of Jacob; that He may instruct us in His ways and that we may walk in His paths." For instruction shall come forth from Zion, the word of the Lord from Jerusalem. Thus He will judge among the nations and arbitrate for the many peoples. And they shall beat their swords into plowshares and their spears into pruning hooks; nation shall not take up sword against nation. They shall never again know war. (Isa. 2:2-4)

The image conveyed here should be construed as an expression of the supremacy of the God of Israel that parallels that of the victorious God(s) of empire, but the victory of the God of Israel is actually a victory only through conceptual absorption. It is a triumphal universal statement couched in the particularist symbolism of Jerusalem. The final result is, indeed, peace, but it is actually an expression of intellectual acrobatics. It is peace along the lines of the *pax romana*, but only a conceptual construct, not one born of actual military and political victory. The text from Micah parallels much of the Isaian passage but adds a surprisingly pluralistic note. The Israelite God, the "Lord of Armies" is responsible, but all peoples are nevertheless seen as walking according to the dictates of their own Gods.

Everyone shall sit under their grapevine or fig tree and with no one to disturb them, for it was the Lord of Hosts who spoke. Though all the peoples walk each in the names of its Gods, we will walk in the name of YHVH our God forever and ever. (Micah 4:4-5)

This is a surprisingly open expression of "inclusive monotheism." Thompson suggests that these and other universalizing poems (Hosea 2, Amos 5 and 9, Micah 5 and 6:2-7:7, and especially Isaiah 44:28-45:13) are positioned in earlier periods by the biblical editors by using a tradition-building technique of story writing known better from Ruth, Jonah, and Esther. The Israelite God is recast as the universal God of heaven.

The underlying doctrine of transcendence is that God is the author of the world, both evil and good, and that he had created it for his own purposes, not those of humanity. History, meaning tradition, reflects his glory. Israel, having committed unforgivable crimes, is forgiven. How else to describe the wonder of the God of mercy?[21]

This monotheism is typified by a merciful God. Previously, the Gods rendered judgment but rarely mercy. In monotheism, however, "[t]he Divine creates and is responsible for both good and evil, but his mercy is without end."[22] Inclusive monotheism existed side by side with a different worldview that Thompson terms "exclusive monotheism." Exclusive monotheism may indeed have emerged under the influence of empire, when authority was centralized through both political and military control, on the one hand, and through religion, on the other. In the worldview of exclusive monotheism, the one true God is at war with the false Gods of all bad things. This notion became dominant in Judea during the tense period followed by the Maccabean revolt against the tremendously successful culture of Hellenism under the Seleucids. The overwhelming appeal of Hellenism and its steamrolling "cultural imperialism" was considered a threat to the very existence of the Judeans and therefore, their culture and religion; but in the second century B.C.E., the Maccabean revolt succeeded in slowing down that threat by establishing a powerful particularism in Israelite—now unambiguously Judean—monotheism.[23]

The Hasmonean period that followed this revolt is known for its syncretism and infighting between the emerging streams of late antique Judaism, which, in turn, increased the tendency toward polemical, exclusivist interpretations of the divine will. Hellenism's appeal and dominance as the "higher culture" needed to be rejected, and this activist monotheistic rejection produced exclusive expressions of monotheism. We observe how the various Jewish interpretive communities that emerged during this period fought against each other as well as against the outside threat of Hellenism. Exclusivist expressions of Judean monotheism would surpass the earlier inclusive monotheism and fight what each believed to be the syncretistic and incorrect position of its competing schools. This would be the legacy of monotheism in general.[24]

Thompson's schema is interesting, but he seems to be suggesting that prior to Hellenism, Israelite monotheism was free from syncretism and competing religious expressions. The Hebrew Bible would seem to indicate otherwise, for it records countless struggles for religious as well as political dominance, from the obvious depictions that we just noted in 2 Kings to more subtle arguments found within the Prophets and in the third division of the Hebrew Bible, "Hagiography."[25] These arguments are so deeply intertwined with political or kinship divisions that they are not always immediately recognizable, but they are certainly there. When one takes a moment to ponder the nature of organized religion as we know it worldwide and then reexamine the world of organized religion depicted by the Bible without romantic inclination, we shouldn't wonder at the evidence indicating religious syncretism and competing religious movements within ancient Israelite religion.

Emerging Religious in a Religious Economy

Thompson's general conclusions are particularly interesting when compared to the most influential current sociological theory of emerging religions. Rodney Stark has been a leader and certainly the most prolific sociologist of religion studying the emergence of new religious movements (NRMs).[26] What follows derives from his study of contemporary emerging religions—not ancient NRMs such as Islam, Christianity, or biblical religion. Nevertheless, some of Stark's observations, with my own extensions, apply directly to our topic of the polemical relationship among monotheisms.[27]

1. NRMs begin when established religions do not speak to the theological and spiritual needs of a significant population of potential consumers.
2. NRMs can form only when there is room in the larger social

and political system for them. They are most likely to succeed when there exists a religious "free market economy."
3. NRMs threaten established religions by their very existence, because they symbolize the failure of established religions to speak to everyone.
4. Whether an NRM begins as a branch or stream within an established religion (sect) or an independent movement (cult), it is opposed by established religions, which feel threatened by the new developments. When the practice or belief system of an internal movement moves beyond the unwritten defining parameters of the established religion out of which it emerges, it becomes a true new religion. Established religions try to control NRMs if they begin within them, or to destroy them if they begin on the outside.
5. NRMs "fight back" through polemical means to demonstrate to an audience of potential believers that they are better expressions of the divine will or provide better spiritual services than establishment religions.

Stark uses the vocabulary of the market economy to describe the emergence of NRMs. A new religious movement is a new "product" in the "religious economy," and those who promote the new product desire to gain "market share" in the "religious consumer market." The promoters—that is, believers and particularly the leadership of NRMs—attempt to "sell" their new product by demonstrating that it will provide better services and give more satisfaction than the traditional products on the market.

Stark conducted his initial studies on new religious movements in the United States and Europe, environments that are overwhelmingly monotheistic and mostly Christian. New religious movements in an overwhelmingly polytheistic environment do not represent such a threat to establishment religions.[28] If there already exist a multitude of deities, or if the conception of deity is one that accepts multiple means of representation, then a new movement would not represent much of a religious threat. (It might represent a political or economic threat if it threatened the established political system or economy through religious affiliation, but for the purposes of this discussion, I must consider this a different topic even though it can be very closely related, as in the case of the emergence of Islam.) A new religious movement or the formation of a sect within polytheistic environments simply adds another God to the pantheon.

This appears to have been the case in the ancient world prior to the rise of monotheism, when multiple expressions of polytheism lived side by side. It is clear that different theisms, whether poly-, heno-, or mono-, have existed side by side for a very long time, because whatever the true reality of the cosmos, our human perceptions tend to be individual, and we can observe this phenomenon long before the modern and postmodern glorification of individual intellectual efforts.

In an overwhelmingly polytheistic world, emerging monotheism would not represent a religious threat. History has demonstrated, however, that once monotheisms have been established, polytheisms *do* represent a significant threat to *them*. Monotheism cannot countenance the existence of multiple Gods. In polytheistic systems, as noted above, various Gods with different names can function similarly or identically—they occupy the same place in the "food chain of divinity." Polytheism by its very nature is inclusive. But if one great God covers all the functions, then any interlopers are existentially threatening. It probably mattered little in early expressions of monotheism as represented in the Hebrew Bible exactly what was the nature of God. Early expressions of monotheism—or to put it differently, early *monotheisms*—were all acceptable to one another because they were articulated and experienced in relation to the overwhelming falseness of polytheisms. It would be self-destructive and probably unimportant to be overly critical of the differences between the monotheistic expressions when the specter of polytheism looms overhead. Therefore, monotheistic believers might disagree about any number of issues, but there was a limit beyond which the arguments would probably not pass.

We know from Josephus and from other literary and archaeological sources that Sadducees, Pharisees, Essenes, and other lesser known groups lived side by side in the late Second Temple period. Those who did not retreat into their own communities, as the Essenic-type groups did, competed with one another openly over political influence, and sometimes nastily, but all were part of an inclusive group of monotheisms that saw themselves as a union in contrast to the polytheistic Greeks and Romans.[29] At some point, however, this multi-monotheistic union would break apart.

By roughly the year "zero," Greco-Romans began to express an increasing interest in the various expressions of monotheism. As Greco-Romans began joining one or another of the monotheisms "on the market," their consumer interest raised the stakes with regard to the differences and identities of the new religious products. Greco-Romans had the option of "shopping" for philosophical schools for centuries, but "better or worse" and "true or false" became important internal categories now also for monotheistic options, because they could mean an increase or decrease in affiliation or support from the huge pool of potential patrons. The question of affiliation raised the stakes because numbers related to political and economic power and influence, and the rise in the political and economic stakes naturally increased the level of polemic.

Internal differences tend to be unimportant when the battle with the outsider is the overwhelming consideration. But when the outside competition of polytheism began to subside, then previously unimportant issues became issues of the day.

Thinking like Greeks and a Stake in the "World to Come"

As more could be gained or lost in the competition between monotheisms, new and more effective tools were sought to enhance one's rating. Two very important innovations entered the Judean universe during this late Second Temple period. One, noted by Thompson, was syllogistic thinking and the search for (capital T) Truth. The second innovation, also acknowledged by students of this period for generations, was a systematic notion of a place in a heavenly World-to-Come that derives from the nature of the individual while in this world.[30] We find neither of these in the Hebrew Bible (with the exception of Daniel 12). Placed together, linear thinking, in combination with the enticement of heaven and the threat of hell, leads to what, extending Thompson's language, might be called *extremely* exclusivist monotheism, one that applied the exclusive attitude toward competing expressions of monotheism as well as toward polytheisms.

During the early period of these emerging innovations, Josephus noted the ideational differences between the Jewish "parties" or "philosophies." He also commented that Essenes and Pharisees believed that the soul was immortal. But there does not seem to be evidence in his works that right thinking merits a heaven or a hell, even among the Essenes, who had a well-developed idea of a world to come of bliss and happiness, and another, "a darksome, stormy abyss, full of punishments that know no end."[31]

Inter-monotheistic polemic intensified and reached its first peak in the "parting of the ways" between Judaism and Christianity. The violent rhetorical battles recorded so clearly in the New Testament and more subtly in the Rabbinic literature of Talmud and Midrash, became emblematic of the relationship between monotheistic religions in general, extending beyond Judaism and Christianity to Islam and its derivatives.

The movements that became Christianity and Rabbinic Judaism emerged out of a spiritual environment that strongly reflected both biblical and Greco-Roman religions and cultures. As they emerged into separate religious movements, they competed fiercely for consumers from the Greco-Roman religious market,[32] and this increased the level of polemic between them. We do not have much of the Jewish polemic because the Jews lost the market to what eventually became a virtual Christian monopoly, after which it became un-politic and eventually illegal to criticize Christians and Christianity in a Christianized Roman Empire. But we have plenty of the Christian polemic, and it became quite shrill.[33]

This Jewish–Christian competition set the tone for all subsequent relations between expressions of monotheism. Once the overwhelming threat of Roman polytheism backed by the state was eliminated, monotheistic believers and their growing institutions no longer needed to tolerate alternate monotheisms. The right expression of the divine will became a matter of great concern—of ultimate concern for some expressions—and that ultimate concern could be expressed as a future eternity in bliss or an eternity in wretched misery. This became more of an issue to Christianities than Judaisms, but that may have been one reason why Christianity captured the market in the fourth century of the common era. To use the economic vocabulary of Stark and his colleagues, what was important was not simply the product but also the brand name.

This terminology may not be an overstatement. The work of John Gager shows that, from the Greco-Roman perspective, the product was simply monotheism. The leading brands were the movements that became Christianity and Rabbinic Judaism. Both movements had similar features: worship of one mighty and universal God, ancient origins, moral-ethical systems, scripture-based traditions, messiahs, and salvation. John Chrysostom's sermons against the Jews were attempts to keep the Greco-Roman consumer pool loyal to his brand of monotheism in the church. He did not want them to be consumers of the Jewish brand of worship as well. His problem was that his parishioners were attending both church and synagogue.[34]

In the course of the polemic, the stakes were raised. When the stakes are low, it matters little what one thinks. But when the risk is the difference between eternal bliss and eternal damnation based on what one thinks or believes, then it matters very much.

This combination is a one-two punch: there is a single religious truth out there that must be realized, and there are serious consequences for realizing or failing to realize that truth. It is well known that the argument was not only between Christianity and Judaism but also between the many different expressions of Christianity.

This nexus may also represent a development that produced a monotheistic "holy war." Prior to the convergence of the notion of right belief with the notion of an afterlife in heaven or hell, there was plenty of violence and strife among Israelites and in the ancient world in general. As noted above, the Hebrew Bible witnesses both religious rivalry and political rivalry couched in religious terms. But the rivalry was clearly and unself-consciously associated with material issues, and the stakes did not include the notions of eternal damnation or bliss. I would suggest that with the convergence of the two notions of right belief and the expectation of reward or punishment in heaven or hell, competition and fighting between groups, even over purely material issues, became articulated increasingly in spiritual terms.[35] The convergence moved conflicts—or more accurately, motivation for engaging in conflicts—from the material to the spiritual-ideological. This is a movement from obvious material motivations of conflict and war to, at the very least, the possibility of ideological motivations.

This transition needs to be explored further, but it may mark the conceptual birth of "holy war" as we have come to know it between and among all three families of monotheistic religion.[36] "Holy war," whether named Crusade, *jihad*, or "commanded war," was always a distinct possibility (and, not infrequently, also a reality) between competing religious expressions *within* as well as *between* the three monotheistic clans. The wars between Sunnis and Shi'is and the Albigensian Crusade mark only two of the best-known examples of "holy war" waged within monotheistic systems. The emergence of Islam followed the basic model described above of a threatening new religious movement that was opposed by the established religions— Meccan idolatry because Islam threatened its intimate economic tie with the lucrative pilgrimage industry,[37] and Medinan Judaism because surviving monotheisms were highly particularist in the seventh-century Middle East. The militant opposition of the Christian Byzantine Empire, both on the battlefield and in the propaganda of the church, helped the Muslims to find their own particularism. However, as with the defining scriptures of the Hebrew Bible and the New Testament, the Qur'an contains both militant and irenic material, either pole of which can be activated by religious scholars when the need arises.

The Unity of Difference

This essay has explored early social-historical motivations for religious competition, polemic, and eventually, war among monotheisms. We have observed how monotheism may have emerged from a paradigm shift caused by the unifying conquests of empire. Even the God of Israel, who was not engaged in any truly successful conquest of empire, assumes the universal image of "God of Armies" (the meaning of "Lord of Hosts"); perhaps because it never actually became a true political empire-God, the God of Israel was the only God of the ancient Near Eastern world that survived the inevitable defeat of empire. As the polytheistic competition gave way to enduring notions of monotheism, these came increasingly into competition and polemical relationships. The increasing particularization was expressed not only in purely theological terms but also through a cultural discourse that was influenced by the languages and worldviews of the Hebrew Bible and ancient Near East, the Greco-Roman world, Persia, and Arabia.

Each of the three "families" of monotheisms, therefore, reflects different anthropologies as well as theologies. Each family is made up of distinct member groups that express unique aspects of the Ineffable, each member group according to its own particular cultural, social, intellectual, and linguistic discourse. The differences are not merely accidents of human culture and history. They reflect what is unique in every one of us who make up the members of our distinctive religious families as we, each by our very createdness, reflect the uniqueness of the Divine Essence.

We rightly strive for a postpolemical age when we can agree to disagree without feeling so threatened that we lash out in violence. Peace and fullness are and should be our grand aspiration, but these will never be achieved by attempting to reduce our particularities. The end of religious diversity is neither desirable nor possible, for it is part of our createdness. But distinctiveness need not be expressed as exclusivity. Monotheism cannot be homogenized, for the unity of the Divine Essence is not a unity that can be reflected adequately in human terms, and certainly not by the example of theological or religious uniformity. The Talmud observes: "This expresses the greatness of the Holy One: a man stamps many coins with one die and they are all alike, but the King of the king of kings, the Holy One, has stamped all humanity with the die of the first Adam, but not one of them is like the other."[38]

Notes

1. This differentiation between an organized and benign universe under the One God in contrast to a fractious and chaotic universe of "the Gods" is actually a presumptive construct that monotheists can agree upon without argument, but it is an a priori assumption. The Hebrew Bible, New Testament, and Qur'an, all of which assume the rule of the One God, also include important passages describing a universe that is on the verge of chaos and destruction.

2. Standard English convention is to capitalize only designations for the monotheistic deity while referring to deities in polytheistic systems in lower case. Because this is, at core, a historical/phenomenological rather than theological study, I prefer to refer to the deity or deities in the same manner.

3. Donald Redford, "The Monotheism of Akhenaten," in *Aspects of Monotheism: How God Is One*, ed. Hershel Shanks and Jack Meinhardt (Washington, D.C.: Biblical Archaeology Society, 1996), 11-26. For a fuller discussion, see Erik Horning, *Akhenaten and the Religion of Light*, trans. David Lorton (Ithaca, N.Y.: Cornell University Press, 1999), 87-94.

4. Ps 8:6; 29:1; 82; 86:8; 89:7; 95:3; 97:7; 135:5; 138:1; 148.

5. Polymnia Athanassiadi and Michael Frede, *Pagan Monotheism in Late Antiquity* (Oxford: Oxford University Press, 1991).

6. Most references are to Abraham the *hanif*. Some note that his monotheism is prior to those of Judaism or Christianity, and Muhammad himself is referred to as a *hanif* on at least one occasion (Q. 2:135; 3:67, 95;

4:125; 6:79; 10:105; 30:30). See Uri Rubin, "*Hanifiyya* and Ka'ba: An Inquiry into the Pre-Islamic Background of *din ibrahim*," *Jerusalem Studies in Arabic and Islam* 13 (1990): 85, 112; Andrew Rippin, "*Rhmnn* and the *hanifs*," in *Islamic Studies Presented to Charles J. Adams*, ed. Wael B. Hallaq and Donald P. Little (Leiden: Brill, 1991), 153-68; Dale Eickelman, "Musaylima: An Approach to the Social Anthropology of Seventh Century Arabia," *Journal of the Economic and Social History of the Orient* 10 (1967): 17-52; Ella Landau-Tasseron, "Unearthing a Pre-Islamic Arabian Prophet," in *Jerusalem Studies in Arabic and Islam* 21 (1997): 42-61; and G. R. Hawting, *The Idea of Idolatry and the Emergence of Islam: From Polemic to History* (Cambridge: Cambridge University Press, 1999).

7. The best recent work on Ugarit and its relationship to biblical religion, which synopsizes all significant prior studies, is Mark S. Smith, *The Origins of Biblical Monotheism: Israel's Polytheistic Background and the Ugaritic Texts* (New York: Oxford University Press, 2001).

8. William G. Dever, "Folk Religion in Early Israel: Did Yahweh Have a Consort?" in *Aspects of Monotheism*, ed. Shanks and Meinhardt, 27-56; Herbert Niehr, "The Rise of YHWH in Judahite and Israelite Religion," in *The Triumph of Elohim: From Yahwisms to Judaisms*, ed. Diana V. Edelman (Grand Rapids: Eerdmans, 1995), 54-55.

9. See Smith, *Origins of Biblical Monotheism*.

10. Niehr, "Rise of YHWH in Judahite and Israelite Religion," 51.

11. N. P. Lemche, *The Canaanites and Their Land: The Tradition of the Canaanites*, Journal for the Study of the Old Testament Supplements 110 (Sheffield: JSOT Press, 1991), 25-62.

12. Karl Jaspers, *Vom Ursprung und Ziel der Geschichte* (Munich: Piper, 1949), cited in S. N. Eisenstadt, *The Origins and Diversity of Axial Age Civilizations* (Albany: State University of New York Press, 1986), 1.

13. Thomas L. Thompson, "The Intellectual Matrix of Early Biblical Narrative: Inclusive Monotheism in Persian Period Palestine," in *The Triumph of Elohim*, ed. Edelman, 113.

14. Ibid., 114.

15. Thompson generalizes far more than the sources would seem to indicate, but he is building a case really for Israel ("Intellectual Matrix," 116).

16. Reuven Firestone, *Jihad: The Origin of Holy War in Islam* (New York: Oxford University Press, 1999); idem, "Holy War Idea in the Biblical Tradition," in *Encyclopedia of Religion and War*, ed. G. Palmer-Fernandez, 1st ed. (New York: Berkshire/Routledge, 2004), 180-85; idem, "Conceptions of

Holy War in Biblical and Qur'anic Tradition," *Journal of Religious Ethics* 24 (1996): 801-24.

17. Diana V. Edelman, "Introduction," in *The Triumph of Elohim*, 20-21.

18. See J. B. Pritchard, ed., *Ancient Near Eastern Texts Relating to the Old Testament* (Princeton, N.J.: Princeton University Press, 1950), 278, 283, 285, 288, 295, 297, 298.

19. Ibid., 307, 310. Whether the unifying process under the Assyrians and Persians resulted in a slightly different relationship of the great God of empire with local national Gods makes little difference to the basic argument.

20. Edelman, "Introduction," in *The Triumph of Elohim*, 22.

21. Thompson, "Intellectual Matrix," 120.

22. Ibid., 122.

23. Elias Bickerman, *From Ezra to the Last of the Maccabees* (New York: Schocken, 1962); Lawrence Schiffman, *From Text to Tradition: A History of Second Temple and Rabbinic Judaism* (New York: Ktav, 1991), 60-79.

24. Thompson, "Intellectual Matrix," 124.

25. Morton Smith, *Palestinian Parties and Politics That Shaped the Old Testament* (1971; reprint, London, SCM Press, 1987).

26. For a recent bibliography of his work, see his *For the Glory of God* (Princeton, N.J.: Princeton University Press, 2003).

27. See Rodney Stark and Laurence R. Iannaccone, "A Supply-Side Reinterpretation of the 'Secularization' of Europe," *Journal for the Scientific Study of Religion* 33 (1994): 230-52; Rodney Stark, "How New Religions Succeed: A Theoretical Model," in *The Future of New Religious Movements*, ed. David G. Bromley and Phillip E. Hammond (Macon, Ga.: Mercer University Press, 1987), 11-19; Rodney Stark and William Sims Bainbridge, *A Theory of Religion* (1987; Rutgers, N.J.: Rutgers University Press, 1996).

28. Rodney Stark, *One True God: Historical Consequences of Monotheism* (Princeton, N.J.: Princeton University Press, 2001), 31-113.

29. Josephus, *The Jewish War*, trans. G. A. Williamson and Rev. E. Mary Smallwood (London: Penguin, 1981), 133-38.

30. George W. E. Nickelsburg, Jr., *Resurrection, Immortality, and Eternal Life in Intertestamental Judaism* (Cambridge, Mass.: Harvard University Press, 1972); J. Edward Wright, *The Early History of Heaven* (Oxford: Oxford University Press, 2000).

31. Josephus, *Jewish War*, 137. That right belief may result in a place in

the World-to-Come later becomes axiomatic in Rabbinic Judaism (Mishnah Sanhedrin, chapter 10).

32. John Gager, *The Origins of Anti-Semitism* (New York: Oxford University Press, 1985).

33. At the top end can be found John Chrysostom's eight sermons *Against the Jews*. For an analysis of the anti-Semitic arguments in these sermons, see Marcel Simon, *Verus Israel: A Study of the Relations between Christians and Jews in the Roman Empire (135-425)*, trans. H. McKeating (London: Littman Library, 1996), 217-23.

34. Gager, *Origins of Anti-Semitism*, 119.

35. Stark argues that not all warring is materialist in origin. Readiness for martyrdom would disprove that, and the Crusades, if material-driven, would have been directed against Spain rather than the Holy Land in the eleventh century (*One True God*, 151-52).

36. James Turner Johnson, *The Holy War Idea in Western and Islamic Traditions* (University Park: Pennsylvania State University Press, 1997); Karen Armstrong, *Holy War: The Crusades and Their Impact on Today's World* (New York: Doubleday, 1988); Majid Khadduri, *War and Peace in the Law of Islam* (Baltimore: Johns Hopkins University Press, 1955); Alfred Morabia, *La Notion de Gihad dans L'Islam Medieval* (Paris, 1975); Rudolf Peters, *Jihad in Classical and Modern Islam* (Princeton, N.J.: Markus Wiener, 1996); Salo Baron and George Wise, *Violence and Defense in the Jewish Experience* (Philadelphia: Jewish Publication Society, 1977); Reuven Firestone, *The Resurrection of Holy War in Modern Judaism* (forthcoming).

37. Not for religious reasons, because from the perspective of the polytheist, veneration of only one God within the system was not considered threatening.

38. Mishnah Sanhedrin 4:5. Note how the designation for God reflects the Achaemenid discourse of "king of kings."

A Problem with Monotheism: Response

Michael L. Fitzgerald

It is with some hesitation that I respond to Professor Firestone's learned paper, yet some observations can be made.

The first regards the *emergence* of monotheism (italics is in the original). There seems to be an adherence to the idea that monotheism evolved out of a primitive polytheism. This would hardly be the Catholic point of view. The *Catechism of the Catholic Church* states, "The desire for God is written in the human heart, because man is created by God and for God, and God never ceases to draw man to Himself" (27). The *Catechism* continues: "In many ways, throughout history down to the present day, men have given expression to their quest for God in their religious beliefs and behavior: in their prayers, sacrifices, rituals, meditations, and so forth. These forms of religious expression, despite the ambiguities they often bring with them, are so universal that one may well call man a *religious being*" (28). These statements correspond to the phrase in the Second Vatican Council's Declaration on the Relationship of the Catholic Church to Other Religions, *Nostra Aetate*:

> Throughout history, even to the present day, there is found among different peoples a certain awareness of a hidden power, which lies behind the course of nature and the events of human life. At times there is present even a recognition of a Supreme Being, or still more of a Father. This awareness and

recognition results in a way of life that is imbued with a deep religious sense. (*Nostra Aetate* §2).

It is granted that this monotheism, to be found in many different forms of traditional religion (i.e., ethnic or tribal religions), may be accompanied by ambiguities. It may not exclude belief in other lesser deities, to whom perhaps more attention may be given than to the Supreme Being. Yet this should not necessarily exclude such religions from being recognized as fundamentally monotheistic. Firestone concedes this through his reference to Akhenaten, though he would prefer to term his reformed-type of religion "henotheism."

In this context a reference is made to the *hanifs*, those in pre-Islamic times who belonged to a monotheistic trend. It is interesting to note that Islam considers monotheism to be innate in the human being, as is shown by the passage in the Qur'an in which the whole of Adam's posterity is represented as testifying to belief in the one Lord. This means that no one can plead ignorance on the Day of Judgment (cf. Q 7:172). Yet human beings tend to forget and, therefore, have to be reminded by revelation that God is one.

Is this not the case with the people of Israel? Professor Firestone appears to give little weight to the experience of the exodus. Can it not be said that the people shaped by this experience were different from the original inhabitants of the land of Canaan? As nomads becoming sedentarized, they tended to adopt the ways of the original population, including their religion, with its cult of fertility gods. Did this not constitute a constant *temptation* for the people of Israel, about which the prophets had continuously to warn? Of course, the attitude to the "gods" is ambiguous. At times their existence seems to be admitted, although they are defeated by the God of Israel. At other times they are considered to be "nothing." The strongest expression for the "exclusive monotheism" to which Israel is called is that of the marriage between God and his people, to the extent that giving worship to any other deity is considered an act of fornication.

A further observation concerns the use that is made of studies on new religious movements (NRMs). It could be wondered whether this is really helpful. Some NRMs are not really new. Certainly in what is known as New Age, what is seen is not a new creation but, among other things, a drawing on ancient traditions such as ancient Egyptian occult practices, or the lore of the Druids, or the polytheism of the ancient Greeks and Romans. Should the idea of NRMs be applied to Christianity and Islam? It is obvious that the "founders" of Christianity and Islam thought of themselves not as starting a new religion but as purifying and fulfilling that which existed already. Jesus continued to go to the temple. Muhammad made a point of performing pilgrimage to the Ka'ba, and this shrine was appointed as the direction of prayer. The consciousness of constituting a new religion came gradually. For Christianity a catalyzing factor was the advent of new adherents who did not belong to the Jewish tradition. For Islam, political factors played a role. The already existing biblical religions were seen to be involved with political powers—the Jews with the Sassanids and the Christians with the Byzantines. So Islam, as a new religion, was also a political movement for Arab independence.

A further minor point. It is strange to see the Pharisees and the Sadducees, together with lesser-known groups, treated as all part of "an inclusive group of monotheisms." The plural here seems odd, since they all surely belonged to the same monotheism, accepting the same God of Israel, even though they differed on certain points.

Again one could wonder whether the clash between Judaism and Christianity is really a competition between monotheisms. It is true that Judaism rejects the fundamental belief of Christianity that God has revealed himself perfectly in Jesus Christ, but Christianity has not rejected the One God as portrayed in the Hebrew Scriptures, as the continued use of these scriptures in the Christian liturgy confirms.

This raises the fundamental question of whether one should talk about "monotheisms" in the plural. This usage leads to the conclusion, common among many people, that the God of the Jews, the God of the Christians, and the God of the Muslims are not the same God. Such a position can lead to a dangerous dismissal of the others and can breed conflict. Is it not wiser, and in fact more conforming to reality, to stress the oneness of God while admitting at the same time that there are different ways of understanding this God?

In his concluding paragraphs Professor Firestone states that the three "families" professing monotheism (it may be remarked in passing that monotheism is not confined to Judaism, Christianity, and Islam, but that is not the point being made here) reflect different anthropologies as well as different theologies, and that the distinct member groups within these families express unique aspects of the Ineffable. It would have been helpful if these interesting observations had been developed further.

A Problem with Monotheism: Response

Mahmoud M. Ayoub

Professor Firestone's interesting essay is, I think, meant to be a challenge to the followers of the reified monotheistic traditions of Judaism, Christianity, and Islam. He wastes no time in making his position known. Professor Firestone entitled his essay "A Problem with Monotheism." He sees the three religions to be at once in dialogue and in dissent. Few can quarrel with this analysis, which is amply borne out by the sad history of their conflicted relations.

In spite of the current problems in the Middle East and those between Muslims and the West in general, the chief aim of interfaith dialogue remains to enhance understanding and peace among the worshipers of Abraham's God. The question that immediately presents itself is to what extent Firestone's essay can help us in our quest for this noble goal. To answer this question fairly, I must critically examine my friend's general methodology and his view of the rise and nature of monotheism in ancient Israel and the role it has played in Judaism, Christianity, and Islam.

Firestone begins with a brief but well-researched analysis of the origins of monotheism. He insists on discussing it strictly within the context of cultural history. He therefore leaves out theology and popular piety, which renders his discussion one-sided. It is a purely secular investigation of an eminently religious phenomenon.

Firestone assumes that historically monotheism arose in an otherwise polytheistic milieu. From the point of view of the history of religion, this view is open to question. The German scholar Wilhelm Schmidt has established in his voluminous work *Der Ursprung der Gottesidee: Eine historisch-kritische und postive Studie* (12 vols.; Münster: Aschendorff, 1912–1955) at least the possibility of the priority of monotheism over polytheism in the rise and development of humankind's religious consciousness. It is more likely that both approaches to the divine developed in parallel ways and similar circumstances. The roots of monotheism were not economic or strictly social, but the human quest for a Supreme Being, or father of human beings and gods. Thus, the concept of "Father Sky" may have developed into the God in heaven (see Mircea Eliade, *Patterns in Comparative Religion*, trans. Rosemary Sheed [Cleveland: World, 1963]).

As for actual influences, it is, for instance, a moot point whether Akhenaten was or was not a monotheist. In spite of the fact that Egypt was the stage of YHWH's "mighty acts" (Exod. 15), YHWH was in no way an Egyptian deity. Therefore the influence of Egyptian theism, whatever its nature, on biblical monotheism appears to be, at best, negligible. The God of ancient Israel was not an urbane Egyptian god but a desert divinity. From the beginning, he appears as a holy power, at once frightening and fascinating, a destroyer and a merciful father. Thus did he appear to Moses in the burning bush and on Mount Sinai (Exod. 3, 4, and 19), to Isaiah in the quaking temple (6:1-13), and to Elijah in the "still small voice" after the storm, thunder, and earthquake (1 Kgs. 19:12).

The ancient Hebrews were, in Firestone's view, "one group of Canaanites that was experimenting with . . . an innovative religious idea that would eventually result in monotheism." Taking into account the general context of Canaanite worship, myths, and rituals, and the violent aversion of the biblical prophets to the whole system, we must ask why, out of all the peoples of the area, did the Hebrews decide to break away from it? Prophets like Amos, Hosea, and Isaiah lived before the sixth century, which Firestone gives as a possible date for the redaction of the Torah and Prophets. This is where theology comes in. There was from the beginning a monotheistic impulse in ancient Israel that triumphed over Canaanite polytheism. This appears to be the view of Yehezkel Kaufmann in his book *The Religion of Israel from Its Beginning to the Babylonian Exile*, trans. Moshe Greenberg (Chicago: University of Chicago Press, 1960).

In the 1950s, a nineteenth-century Lebanese shepherd monk was recognized as a saint with many miracles to his credit. More Muslims than Christians flocked to his shrine for healing and blessing. Until Mar Sharbil was canonized by the Catholic Church during the Lebanese civil war (1975–1991), he was the saint of Lebanese Christians and Muslims alike. But once he was canonized as a saint of the Catholic Church, the Muslims rejected him. I believe that the Sharbil story can serve as a good model of the rise and development of Israelite monotheism in its Canaanite environment. There, too, it was a case of pietistic interactions encountering the social and spiritual needs of a diverse society. No doubt, archaeological research can provide us with valuable information surrounding such a tremendous religious transformation, but it cannot tell us what went on in people's hearts and minds. Like the recognition of Sharbil, allegiance to one God in a multicultural, and even polytheistic, environment can be scrutinized and imagined historically, but such approaches are unable to capture or penetrate the mysterious origins of singular religious phenomena.

Firestone seems to allow for the possibility of the rise of Israelite monotheism during the "Axial Age" (eighth to second centuries B.C.E.). This is, in my view, quite plausible, given the great religious transformations that took place in all parts of the known world during this rich period. For a religious historian of religion like me, this is a case of divine intervention to guide humanity to a clearer knowledge of God. Within this general theological principle we can place all monotheistic developments, whether in Greek philosophy and Hellenistic culture or early Christianity and Rabbinic Judaism. Islam became heir to this great legacy.

I know I am proposing a different methodology from that of Professor Firestone. I am arguing that religions emerged in a particularly rich spiritual and cultural environment, while he places the emergence of religions in a "religious economy." I need not review his interesting use of the work of Rodney Stark and other sociologists of religion and biblical scholars. I only wish to indicate that Stark applied his market-economy theories to the rise of religious movements in modern times. The validity of applying these theories to societies of the ancient world is, I believe, open to question. I must say, the whole idea sounds very strange.

Having said all this, I agree with Firestone's conclusion, to which I will come at the end of this review. If we see all religious developments, including monotheism, in their proper historical context, we can more easily demystify them. Religiosity is always two-dimensional. It is the human quest for Truth, and divine guidance to it. We cannot make sense of one without the other.

As a Muslim, I believe that the absolute and transcendent Truth (*al-haqq*) is God. All religions are ways to the Truth, but they are not the Truth. This is to say, our religions are relative approaches to the absolute Truth. This should help us not to make absolute claims for that which is relative. Religions are relative only in relation to the transcendent and ultimate reality. In themselves they are true; otherwise they have no value, and thus cannot serve as a framework for humankind's faith and hope.

Firestone has little to say about Islam. However, he applies the same consumer principles to the rise of Islam as well. Again, I feel that such applications can at best provide limited explanations. He rightly sees all conflicts, "holy war ... Crusade, *jihad*, or commanded war," as realities reflecting competing religious expressions, both within and among the three monotheistic clans. As a way out, Professor Firestone calls on all of us "to strive for a postpolemical age, when we can agree to disagree without lashing out in violence." I hope that this goal can be realized without our having to debunk our faiths and history.

It matters not when and how such stories were redacted into the Hebrew Bible. What matters is that long before and long after their inclusion in the Jewish and Christian Scriptures they have nourished the piety and religious imagination of countless Jews, Christians, and Muslims.

A Problem with Monotheism: REPLY

Reuven Firestone

FOR JEWS, the worst and most disastrous misfortune of their history (until the Holocaust) was not the destruction of the First Temple by the Babylonians with its ending of the beloved Davidic kingdom and the beginning of heartbreaking exile by the waters of Babylon. Nor was it the horrific and final destruction of the Second Temple by the pagan Romans, who leveled the holy place and demonstrated to the world the triumph of idolatry over monotheism. To be sure, these were both horrific experiences that left huge wounds in the heart of the Jewish people. But the worst premodern disaster for the Jews was the failure of its great militant messianic movement. Led spiritually by its most dearly loved Rabbi Akiba, and militarily by its messianic general Bar Koziba (Kokhba), the failure of the "Bar Kokhba Rebellion" resulted in the deaths of countless numbers of innocents through the methodical eradication of the Judeans by the Roman legions, the horrible torture of its leaders, and even the outlawing of *semikhah*—the ordination of rabbis. This fiasco, which occurred in the first half of the second century, forced the Jews into a retreat that was never reversed, neither under pagan Rome nor under the Christian Roman Empire of Byzantium.

But in retrospect many centuries later, it may be that the worst disaster for the Jews became one of the most important milestones for Judaism. It forced a tremendous and unprecedented act of deep personal and communal retrospection. The result was an end to triumphalism: the necessity to jettison so many simple and simplistic assumptions about God and the Almighty's relationship to humanity in general, and to the Jewish people in particular. The absolute failure of force of arms in the attempt at messianic salvation forced a level of unprecedented humility upon both the individual and the corporate body and compelled Jews to rethink their relationships with the individual, the Jewish community, and the larger world population of nonbelievers. The result of near-disaster was a "re-tooling" of religion. The range of Judaism(s) of the rabbis, as exemplified by the Talmud and Midrash and their related literatures, is more compassionate, sophisticated, and certainly more mature than what had been previously known. I should clarify that the literatures and theologies expressed in the Hebrew Bible are by no means simple—in fact, they are often extraordinarily sophisticated. But they tend to view the world in a binary fashion that is transcended by the Judaism emergent after Bar Kokhba. Rabbinic Judaism is exemplified by the struggle to deal with the extreme complexity and uncertainty of real life, unsullied by overly simplistic assumptions and fantastic constructions of the world. It is a religion that, although never again a major player in the politics of world affairs, learned successfully how to come to terms with the world as it really is.

For Christians, the worst and most disastrous calamity of their history was not the Islamic conquest that took Christendom's most precious spiritual possessions in the Holy Land and its most important economic holdings in the fruitful Nile Valley. Nor was it the collapse and incapacity of the Crusades to regain the birthplace of Christianity in Bethlehem, Galilee, and Jerusalem. It was, rather, the failure of Christians to hold together in their own Christian continent of Europe, a land that, for most of the last two millennia, remained virtually entirely Christian! The failure of a single, universal Christian faith to find common meaning among all Christians resulted in the deaths of countless innocents in Europe in its religious wars, and the uprooting of even more families, who lost their livelihoods and often starved or sold themselves into servitude for survival. Christians would never again feel the comfort of belonging to a universal faith, as the very fabric of the community was rent asunder, never again to be rejoined.

But in retrospect many centuries later, it may be that the worst disaster for Christians as a unified religious community became one of the most important milestones for Christianity. It forced the reevaluation of long-held assumptions that often simply did not conform to reality. It required a redistribution of power and authority. It demanded deep introspection among its adherents, both within the Catholic Church and among the many new religious sects and movements. It compelled Christians as individuals and as members of church communities to reevaluate the meaning of individual and communal salvation and finally, after centuries, to reevaluate in a more charitable way the place of non-Christians in a world that might not inevitably lead to Christ.

For Muslims, the worst and most disastrous catastrophe of their history was not the end of the virtuous caliphate of the first, righteous caliphs, after which corrupt dynastic rule tore apart the fabric of Islamic idealism and the spirit of the new movement. Neither was it the Mongol invasion, with its destruction of the caliphate altogether in the thirteenth century, replacing the Muslim leader of the Islamic world with a pagan idolater. These things weakened the spiritual dynamism of the world Muslim community, to be sure, and caused deep splits that have enervated it severely. But it has always recovered and then reconsidered itself to be, as Jews and Christians considered themselves before and often also now, the elite of the monotheistic faiths and the only truly perfect expression of the divine will. In fact, however, the greatest challenge to Muslims in their long and glorious history is occurring right now. It is exemplified by their failure in the modern era, in the name of any and every social system, including Islam, to compete with Western and now also other non-Western nations and communities, many of which are seen by Muslims to be not only unbelievers but idolaters. This has resulted in huge numbers of innocent deaths in aborted uprisings and revolutions, counterrevolutions, civil wars, and acts of terror *within* as well as outside of Muslim countries. Internal violence has surged beyond borders and brought on more pain from both East and West through economic reprisals, embargoes, and war. It has been and continues to be an existential calamity of unprecedented proportions that affects millions upon millions of believers.

But in retrospect, if we could jump ahead some centuries from now, it may be that this worst disaster for Muslims will prove to be one of the most important milestones for Islam. Had God wished, God could certainly have made known the divine Truth in a manner that could be grasped equally by all humanity. But God did not. If ever there was a Truth with a capital T, it is the uncertainty that is endemic to existence, its meaning, its purpose, and its outcome. As collective faith communities, all have met with or are currently confronting calamities of unprecedented proportions. In fact, all have had the privilege of confronting calamitous uncertainty a number of times in history.

Our confrontations with humanly wrought disasters have resulted in shock that we should allow to penetrate to the deepest depth of our souls. Sometimes we have managed to allow the shock to penetrate. Sometimes we have not. Perhaps such disasters are God's mysterious way of telling us to wake up. Violence and evil are not God's design, but they most certainly demonstrate God's toleration of the human will, to offer not only succor and solace but also misery and pain.

Monotheism, by its very nature as an expression of the divine essence, offers one of the most sincere expressions of compassion and comfort to humanity. But history has proven that the hardest expressions of human cruelty have also fit over religion like an overlay across a map. One can see the original map through the overlay, but the overlay changes the perspective and offers an entirely different way of looking at the original core.

"Getting back to basics" often provides its own overlay and may not be a return to pure religion at all. Who can truly know that one's own belief captures the divine Truth? Monotheist communities who have not yet must now stop assuming that *their* understanding of God is the single source for happiness on earth and salvation in a world to come.

One of my favorite scriptural expressions of what I believe and pray is the divine will is found in Qur'an 5:48: "For every one We have appointed a divine law and custom. If God had wished, He would have made you all one religious nation, but [God chose not to do that in order] to try you by what He has given you. So vie with one another in doing good works! Unto God you must all return, and He will then inform you of how you differ."

3

Relations among the Abrahamic Religions
A Catholic Point of View

MICHAEL L. FITZGERALD

AN OLD ADAGE RUNS *lex orandi, lex credendi*: the rule of prayer indicates the rule of belief. Following this, I wish to begin with a quotation from one of the most sacred expressions of prayer in the Western Catholic tradition, namely, the First Eucharistic Prayer, or the Roman Canon of the Mass. After the consecration of the bread and wine, which thus become transformed into the Body and Blood of Jesus Christ, the chief celebrant offers these gifts to God the Father, saying: "Look with favor on these offerings and accept them as once you accepted the gifts of your servant Abel, the sacrifice of Abraham, our father in faith, and the bread and wine offered by your priest Melchizedek." The liturgy thus links the new sacrifice of Jesus Christ, "the blood of the new and everlasting covenant," with certain figures of the First Testament, Abel, Abraham, and Melchizedek, whose offerings were acceptable to God.

What is important to note is the way Abraham is described: "our father in faith." This is the key to the Catholic understanding of Abraham, which will form the first section of this paper. Then will follow a brief exposition of the relations of the Catholic Church to Judaism and to Islam, respectively. Some considerations can then be offered on dialogue among these religions, bilateral, trilateral, and multilateral. Finally, it may be useful to return to the figure of Abraham to gather some inspiration from his example.

The Catholic Understanding of Abraham

It should be recalled first of all that Christianity accepts the First Testament as part of its own revelation.[1] Therefore, all that is said about Abraham in the Book of Genesis, but also in Wisdom and in Ben Sira, is accepted as the word of God. It is not necessary to repeat the information given in these books. The aim here is to give the specific Catholic understanding of the figure of Abraham. For this purpose, we will have recourse to a Catholic compendium, *The Catechism of the Catholic Church*.[2] At times references will be made to various books of the New Testament.

The call of Abraham is seen as an important element in God's plan of salvation for humankind. "In order to gather together scattered humanity, God calls Abram from his country, his kindred and his father's house, and makes him Abraham, that is 'the father of a multitude of nations.' 'In you all the nations of the earth shall be blessed'" (Gen. 12:3) (*CCC* §59). The blessing given to Abraham will be one of the constant themes of the scriptures. Attention is nevertheless turned to the way the promise of descendants is understood: "The people descended from Abraham ... the chosen people ... would be the root onto which the Gentiles would be grafted, once they believed" (*CCC* §60) (cf. Rom. 11:17-18, 24).

The final words of this quotation, "once they believed," are to be noted. Abraham is presented above all as a model of faith. Here the *CCC* follows the meditation of the author of the Letter to the Hebrews. Abraham proved his faith in God by his obedience. He obeyed when he was called to leave his home "not knowing where he was to go." He lived by faith as a stranger and pilgrim in the promised land. It was by faith that Sarah, Abraham's wife, was given the possibility of conceiving the son of the promise. It was by faith, too, that

Abraham was ready to offer this son in sacrifice (*CCC* §145) (cf. Heb. 11:8-12, 17-19).

Abraham is also given as a model of hope (*CCC* §165). For the promise of a child was made to him when "he was about a hundred years old—and Sarah too old to become a mother" (Rom 4:19). Yet this did not deter him. "Though it seemed Abraham's hope could not be fulfilled, he hoped, and he believed, and through doing so he did become the father of many nations exactly as he had been promised" (Rom. 4:18).

Abraham's hope, based on faith, included faith in the resurrection. He believed that God could bring life from what was practically a dead body. This faith also upheld him when he was asked to sacrifice his son: "It was by faith that Abraham, when put to the test, offered up Isaac. He offered to sacrifice his only son even though the promises had been made to him and he had been told: 'It is through Isaac that your name will be carried on.' He was confident that God had the power even to raise the dead; and so, figuratively speaking, he was given back Isaac from the dead" (Heb. 11:17-19).[3]

Jesus, of course, as Paul observes, is born subject to the Law given to Moses. "When the appointed time came, God sent his Son, born of a woman, born a subject of the Law, to redeem the subjects of the Law and to enable us to be adopted as sons" (Gal. 4:4-5). Jesus' circumcision, on the eighth day after his birth, "is the sign of his incorporation into Abraham's descendants, into the people of the covenant. It is a sign of his submission to the Law" (*CCC* §527). Yet the whole burden of the Christian message is that the Law can no longer save and that salvation is in Jesus Christ. "The Law, the sign of God's promise and covenant, ought to have governed the hearts and institutions of that people to whom Abraham's faith gave birth" (*CCC* §709). But infidelity to the covenant called for "a promised restoration, according to the Spirit" (*CCC* §710).

It is therefore faith that saves. Because Abraham believed, "this faith was considered as justifying him" (Rom. 4:3). "Because he was 'strong in his faith,' Abraham became the 'father of all who believe'"

(*CCC* §146; cf. Rom. 4:11, 18, 20). The primacy of faith over descent is stressed elsewhere in the New Testament. John the Baptist tells those who have come to listen to his preaching: "Do not presume to tell yourselves, 'We have Abraham as father,' because I tell you, God can raise children for Abraham from these stones" (Matt. 3:9). A commentator on this Gospel puts it succinctly: "Salvation is not hereditary."[4] The same idea comes out in Jesus' polemic with the Jews who wished to kill him. He said to them: "If you were Abraham's children you would do as Abraham did" (John 8:39). Nor is faith confined to the descendants of Abraham. Jesus praises the faith of a Roman centurion and remarks: "I tell you solemnly, nowhere in Israel have I found faith like this. And I tell you that many will come from the east and west to take their places with Abraham, Isaac and Jacob at the feast in the kingdom of heaven" (Matt. 8:10-11).

For those who follow the example of Abraham, faith in the resurrection is also important. It has been remarked that Abraham's faith was considered as justifying him. Paul observes: "Scripture however does not refer only to him but to us as well when it says that his faith was thus 'considered'; our faith too will be 'considered' if we believe in him who raised Jesus our Lord from the dead, Jesus who was put to death for our sins and raised to justify us" (Rom. 4:23-25).

To sum up, Catholic doctrine teaches that Abraham is truly a father figure. He is the father of the chosen people, but above all he is the ancestor of Jesus Christ, who is the ultimate bearer of the promise made to Abraham. The patriarch—for this is how Christians look upon Abraham—is also presented as a model. He submitted to God's will, even though he did not understand it. He put his trust in God, with whom, one could say, he had a confident relationship (it will be necessary to return to this aspect in the final section of this paper). For Christians, Abraham is "our father in faith."

The Catholic Church and Judaism

The Declaration *Nostra Aetate* of the Second Vatican Council radically renewed the outlook of the Catholic Church on Judaism. It is interesting to note that paragraph 4 of this document, which deals with Judaism, starts immediately with a reference to Abraham. It recalls "the spiritual ties which link the people of the New Covenant to the stock of Abraham." By the use of the phrase "stock of Abraham" the physical descent of the Jews from Abraham is recognized. In contrast, Christians as "the people of the New Covenant" have only "spiritual ties" with them. The declaration marks both continuity and discontinuity.

On the side of continuity there is the fact that the beginnings of the faith and election of the church are to be found in the history of the chosen people, "in the patriarchs, Moses and the prophets." It is recognized, therefore, that Christians, "who as men of faith are sons of Abraham, are included in the patriarch's call." The church, and its mission of salvation, is mystically prefigured in this history, particularly in the exodus. Moreover, the church cannot forget that it has received the revelation of the First Testament through the people with whom God established the "ancient covenant." The words of Paul to the Romans are quoted: "They are Israelites, and to them belong the sonship, the glory, the covenants, the giving of the law, the worship, and the promises; to them belong the patriarchs, and of their race according to the flesh, is the Christ" (Rom. 9:4-5). It is further stated that "Paul maintains that the Jews remain very dear to God, for the sake of the patriarchs, since God does not take back the gifts he bestowed or the choice he made." The church of the Gentiles, the Nations, has been grafted onto this root, and this gives rise to a living and life-giving bond. The books of the First Testament continue to nourish Christians; they are used constantly in the church's liturgy. Here again one could say *lex orandi, lex credendi*.

Yet there is also discontinuity. Although Jesus and his first disciples were Jews, "Jews for the most part did not accept the Gospel." So there came about a separation that will continue until that day, which the church awaits, "when all people will call on God with one voice."

In the meantime Jews and Christians are exhorted to cultivate a relationship of understanding and appreciation. It is enjoined on

Christians to avoid offensive language. Jews are not to be spoken of as "rejected or accursed." There is strong reprobation for any form of persecution, for any display of anti-Semitism. Common studies are encouraged, both of the Bible and of theological questions. One could apply to Jewish–Christian relations the exhortation given in more general terms in paragraph 2 of *Nostra Aetate*: "to enter with prudence and charity into discussion and collaboration with members of other religions. Let Christians, while witnessing to their own faith and way of life, acknowledge, preserve and encourage the spiritual and moral truths found among non-Christians, also their social life and culture."

The mention of witness here is important. In dialogue, partners must remain true to their own identity. This is true for Christians also. It is not surprising, therefore, that the final paragraph of the section on Judaism restates the belief that Christ has died for the salvation of all, including the Jews, and so there is a duty for the church "to proclaim the cross of Christ as the sign of God's universal love and the source of all grace."

This summary of the teaching of *Nostra Aetate* illustrates, I would hope, the solid basis that Vatican II has given for Jewish–Christian relations. Yet it is evident that difficulties subsist, in particular with regard to the relationship between the "ancient covenant" and the "New Covenant," and also concerning the concept of mission. Before giving further consideration to these points, it may be useful to call attention to the first document published with the aim of facilitating the application of the teaching of the council: *Guidelines for Implementing* Nostra Aetate §4 (1974).[5]

The *Guidelines* acknowledge both the debt of Christianity to Judaism and the widening gap between the two. It is stated that Christians "must strive to learn by what essential traits the Jews define themselves in the light of their own religious experience." An important principle of interreligious dialogue is at stake here. People must be allowed to "define themselves." They are not to suffer from a projection imposed on them by people who do not share their faith. In terms of Judaism, one cannot understand the living reality of the Jewish faith from the First Testament alone, as if it were something static, frozen at the time of Jesus and the birth of the church. On the contrary, Judaism is to be recognized as an independent and developing religion.

This document goes on to outline for Catholics certain areas that need attention. It encourages *dialogue* with a view to increasing mutual knowledge. In this process there should be no forgoing of one's own identity. For Christians this means that Christ has to be preached, but following the principles laid down by the conciliar Declaration on Religious Liberty, *Dignitatis humanae*, which states clearly that truth is to be proposed, never imposed. With regard to *liturgy* it is considered important to note the elements derived from Jewish worship. Since Vatican II has encouraged greater use of readings from the First Testament, it is considered important to develop a proper understanding of these texts. In the translations the texts are not to be altered on account of difficulties they might raise, but care is to be taken in preaching that the meaning of the texts not be distorted. In the realm of *education* the acceptance of Judaism as a developing tradition and a distinct religion is accentuated. Yet there is a warning against creating false oppositions between Judaism and Christianity, such as considering the former to be the religion of the law and the latter the religion of love. Encouragement is given to cooperation among scholars and the establishment of chairs of Jewish studies in Catholic universities. Finally, there is a call for *social action*, common endeavors for justice and peace and the good of humankind at all levels.

Let me turn now to the first of the difficulties mentioned above, namely, the understanding of covenant or covenants. Paul, in the passage quoted from Romans, uses this term in the plural, thus covering both the covenant with Abraham and that of Sinai.[6] Yet the contrast lies mainly between the terms used by *Nostra Aetate*, "ancient covenant" and "New Covenant."[7] Pope John Paul II, in an oft-quoted speech to Jews, given in Mainz, Germany, on November 17, 1980, spoke of the dialogue between Judaism and Christianity and said: "The first dimension of this dialogue, that is the meeting between the people of God of the Old Covenant, never revoked by God (cf. Rom. 11:29), is at the same time a dialogue within our Church, that is to say, between the first and the second part of the Bible." Much ink has been spent trying to elucidate the consequences of this nonrevocation. Norbert Lohfink, in a little book entitled *The Covenant Never Revoked*, refers to "one covenant theories," "two covenant theories," and "many covenant theories."[8] He points to the difficulty of speaking about the "old" and the "new," for if the new replaces the old the Jews are left with no covenant at all. Nor would it be correct to speak of the "old" covenant for the Jews and the "new" for the Nations, for there were Jews too in the New Covenant. For Lohfink, "one ought not to speak of 'two covenants' or even of several 'covenants,' but only of one covenant. The formulation 'a twofold way to salvation' can be supported. But this must be understood 'dramatically.'"[9] History shows us that there is a possibility of guilt, freedom, repentance, reconciliation, and thus of "dramatic action." There are not two parallel ways, one for Israel and the other for the Nations. God has only one plan of salvation, and at the end he will be "one."[10] How is this tension between the permanent validity of the covenant with the chosen people and the universal salvific significance of the death and resurrection of Jesus to be overcome? In a later speech, addressing the Anti-Defamation League of B'nai B'rith in 1984, John Paul II said: "the respect we speak of is based on the mysterious spiritual link which brings us close together, in Abraham and, through Abraham, in God who chose Israel and brought forth the Church from Israel." Eugene Fisher comments:

> Here, there is not the slightest hint of supersessionism or of that subtler form of triumphalism that would envision Israel as having exhausted its salvific role "in giving birth" to Christianity. The mystery, in the pope's profound vision, lies much deeper than any such "either/or" theological dichotomies can reach. It is precisely such a "both/and" approach that the pope is calling Catholic scholars and educators to develop today.[11]

If the covenant with Israel is still valid, does this mean that the church has no mission to Jews? Certain statements would seem to point in this direction. That made in the United States by the National Councils of Synagogues and Delegates of the Bishops' Committee on Ecumenical and Interreligious Affairs aroused much controversy. More recently the final communiqué of the meeting between the Chief Rabbinate of Israel and the Holy See's Commission for Religious Relations with Jews (CRRJ) stated: "Dialogue is a value in itself and excludes any intention of converting."[12] Again this provoked strong reaction from some Catholics. A document published by the Holy See's Pontifical Council for Interreligious Dialogue, *Dialogue and Proclamation*, is relevant here. It states that "interreligious dialogue does not merely aim at mutual understanding and friendly relations. It reaches a much deeper level, where exchange and sharing consist in a mutual witness to one's beliefs and a common exploration of one's respective religious convictions.... Given this aim, a deeper conversion of all toward God, interreligious dialogue possesses its own validity." So conversion of the other to one's own religion is not the aim of dialogue, though this may happen. The document continues: "In this process of conversion (to God), 'the decision may be made to leave one's own previous spiritual or religious situation in order to direct oneself toward another.' Sincere dialogue implies, on the one hand, mutual acceptance of differences, or even of contradictions, and on the other, respect for the free decision of persons made according to the dictates of their conscience (cf. *Dignitatis Humanae* §2)."[13]

Cardinal Kasper, the president of the CRRJ, tackled the thorny question of mission in a talk given at Boston College, November 7, 2002. He stated boldly that "the word 'mission' is central in the New Testament. We cannot cancel it, and if we should try to do so, it would not help the Jewish–Christian dialogue at all. Rather it would make the dialogue dishonest, and ultimately distort it." He proposed, however, a distinction. "Mission understood as a call to conversion from idolatry to the living and true God (1 Thess. 1:9) does not apply and cannot be applied to Jews. They confess the living true God, who gave and gives them support, hope, confidence and strength in many difficult situations of their history." Therefore, concludes the cardinal, there can be "no organized Catholic missionary activity towards the Jews." On the other hand, Christians are called to give witness to Jesus Christ, even to Jews.

> The universality of Christ's redemption for Jews and for Gentiles is so fundamental throughout the entire New Testament ... that it cannot be ignored or passed over in silence.... This does not mean that Jews in order to be saved have to become Christians; if they follow their own conscience and believe in God's promises as they understand them in their religious tradition they are in line with God's plan, which for us comes to its historical completion in Jesus Christ.

For Christians, adds Kasper, mission "includes giving testimony of Jesus the Christ to all and in all places; for Christians this is the mandate of Jesus Christ himself (Mt 28:19). They cannot renounce doing so without renouncing to be Christians."[14]

The Catholic Church and Islam

The relations among the Abrahamic religions are asymmetrical. Christianity accepts the Hebrew Bible as the first part of its own scriptures, as a part of revelation. But Judaism naturally does not accept the New Testament. Were Jews to recognize the New Testament as revelation from God they would become Christians. Similarly Islam considers the Torah to have been "sent down" by God to the Jews, and the gospel to have been "sent down" to Christians, but Jews and Christians do not accept the Qur'an as revelation from God. If they did, they would become Muslims. The difference in attitude is a reflection of separate identities.

Yet there is a further difference in the way Christians relate to what they term the Old Testament, and the attitude of Muslims to the scriptures that preceded the Qur'an. For Christians the Old Testament is an integral part of their own scriptures, and this is shown, for example, by the use of readings from the Old Testament in Christian worship. Texts from the Old Testament or the New Testament would never form part of *salat*, the Islamic ritual prayer. Here again the validity of the adage *lex orandi, lex credendi* is verified.

The question that must occupy us here, however, is not how Muslims view Christianity but rather how the Catholic Church views Islam. After some rapid indications on positions current before Vatican II, we will examine the teaching of the council.[15]

Islam was often considered a heresy. This was the position of John Damascene (675–753) in the century following the rise of Islam. Muhammad is said to have been influenced by Christians and to have "formed a heresy of his own." It could be observed that, strictly speaking, it is certainly unjustified to consider Islam in this way. As defined by canon law, heresy is "the obstinate post-baptismal denial of some truth which must be believed with divine and catholic faith" (c. 751). To become a heretic one must first belong to the church. This obviously does not apply to Muhammad.

Islam was also treated as a false religion, for example, by George Harmatolos, writing in the Byzantine Empire in the ninth century. In his history of mankind he dedicates a chapter to Islam, comparing it unfavorably with Christianity. He states that it is a religion that springs from a false prophet. This position could be criticized as coming from prejudice.

Even worse, Islam has been seen as satanic. A "monk of France," possibly Hugh of Cluny (1049–1119), wrote in this vein to the Muslim king of Saragossa, inviting him to embrace the Christian faith. Islam was seen as something diabolical, because it prevented God's saving work from being accomplished. It could be said that this opinion was quite common in missionary circles up to the Second Vatican Council.

Thomas Aquinas (1225-1274) appears to have categorized Muslims as unbelievers, the term "believer" being reserved to one who shared the Christian faith. His *Summa contra gentiles* was composed to help those of his order, the Dominicans, who were preaching to Jews and Muslims. He wrote a shorter work, *De rationibus fidei contra Saracenos, Graecos et Armenos ad Cantorem Antiochenum,* in which he gave advice about entering into disputations with unbelievers. Thomas does not treat Islam as a corrupt version of Christianity but, implicitly at least, as a separate religion. His position is perhaps the foundation for viewing Islam as a natural religion.

In contrast to Christianity with its mysteries and dogmas, Islam has been praised as a religion accessible to all. This is the view found in the writings of Voltaire and Thomas Carlyle. Some Catholic theologians have also been inclined to see Islam as a natural religion, since it remains, in its approach to God, at the level of what can be known by reason alone. George Anawati, a Dominican like Thomas, qualified this assertion. For him, Islam was a natural religion insofar as the truths it professes are accessible to reason, yet for Muslims it is a revealed religion, since they hold these truths to have been revealed by God. This would seem to conform to the Islamic view of itself as the religion of *fitra,* that is, the religion given by God to humanity at its very creation. Prophetic revelation, culminating in the mission of Muhammad, serves to remind human beings of this natural religion.

The distinguished Islamicist Louis Massignon (1883–1962) was perhaps the first Catholic to present Islam as an Abrahamic religion. He emphasized the role of Ishmael, "excluded," driven out into the desert but enjoying a special blessing. This blessing has been renewed, as it were, through Muhammad, so that Islam could be considered an "Abrahamic schism" before the foundation of Judaism and Christianity. Its role is to goad Jews and Christians to return to the correct understanding of their own religions. It could be remarked here that this position, generous though it may seem, does not consider Islam in itself but only its function with respect to the religions preceding it.

Nevertheless, Massignon's more open attitude toward Islam prepared the way for the teaching of the Second Vatican Council on this point, though he did not live to see the beginning of the council. Of course, it has often been said that the Second Vatican Council spoke about Muslims rather than about Islam. This is true insofar as the council did not intend to give a full description of Islam, entering into a detailed discussion of what could be conceived as the positive and negative aspects of this religion. The statement in *Lumen Gentium* (§16) is very succinct and thus can be quoted in its entirety: "But the plan of salvation also includes those who acknowledge the Creator, in the first place among whom are the Muslims: these profess to hold the faith of Abraham, and together with us they adore the one, merciful God, mankind's judge on the last day." In some ways paragraph 3 of *Nostra Aetate* could be considered an extended commentary on these lines, going on to draw out some practical consequences for relations between Christians and Muslims.

It should be noted, nevertheless, that *Nostra Aetate* does speak about religions, and these general affirmations should be held to refer also to Islam. The religions, as has been said, provide answers for the fundamental questions of human existence (see *Nostra Aetate* §1). Nothing that is true and holy in religions is rejected by the church. Consequently, the church gives encouragement to its members to enter into a dialogue of exchange and collaboration with the members of other religions (see *Nostra Aetate* §2). On this basis then, an examination can be made regarding what the council says, at least by way of implication, about Islam as a religion.

Islam is treated first of all as a monotheistic religion. This is not surprising, for belief in the one God is a fundamental characteristic of Islam, forming the first part of the profession of faith and constituting the main burden of Islamic theology, as bears witness its name, *tawhîd* (establishing or defending the oneness of God). Yet noteworthy are the words in the text of *Lumen Gentium* according to which Muslims *together with us* adore the one, merciful God. Though such a statement may be opposed by both Christians and Muslims—by some Christians, because Muslims do not believe in the Trinity, and by some Muslims because Christians are considered to be unbelievers (*kuffâr*) precisely because of their belief in the Trinity—the affirmation *together with us* remains. As Christians and

Muslims, we understand God differently, but we do not worship different divinities, since God is one. Our religions are truly monotheistic.[16]

A further reflection would appear to be appropriate. The conciliar texts on Islam speak about belief in God as Creator and Judge. This is also something that Christians and Muslims have in common. It is not to be overlooked since it has practical consequences, providing an opening for dialogue on the common origin and common destiny of humankind. It can also lead to a joint evaluation of the role of human beings as vice-regents (*khulafa*) or stewards of God's creation, with implications for a more equitable distribution and respectful use of the earth's resources. Such a reflection is not going beyond the conciliar basis, since *Nostra Aetate* exhorts Christians and Muslims to work together to "preserve and promote peace, liberty, social justice and moral values" (*Nostra Aetate* §3).

Muslims often use the term "celestial" as applied to the three religions, Judaism, Christianity, and Islam. They have a celestial origin because they claim to be based on revelation. It may be asked whether the texts of the council encourage Catholics to accept this terminology. In *Nostra Aetate*, after the reference to Muslims' belief in God who is one and the Creator, there is added "who has also spoken to men." As Robert Caspar has written:

> This divine name, the God who reveals, is of capital importance for the religious and supernatural value of the Islamic faith. The Muslim does not merely believe in a God of reason, a "God of philosophers" as Pascal put it, but in a living God, "the God of Abraham, Isaac and Jacob," a God who has spoken to men, within their history, by men, the prophets, even if Christians and Muslims have a different idea of the identity and role of these prophets.[17]

An amendment had been proposed adding the words *homines per prophetas allocutum*, but this was not accepted. The theological commission decided to omit the reference to the prophets, since it was felt to be ambiguous. The church might be giving the impression of accepting the prophetic role of Muhammad. Obviously Christians do not recognize Muhammad as a prophet in the way Muslims do, that is, as the final prophet bringing the definitive revelation—otherwise they would become Muslims. On the other hand, Muslims have difficulty in accepting any type of qualified prophetic role that Christians would be ready to attribute to Muhammad. Therefore silence was preferred on this point and the text remained: "who has also spoken to men," without specifying how God speaks to humanity. This silence has been maintained in the official documents of the church. The church's constant teaching is that after Jesus Christ there is no further need of revelation. "The Christian dispensation, therefore, as the new and definitive covenant, will never pass away, and we now await no further new public revelation before the glorious manifestation of our Lord Jesus Christ" (*Dei Verbum* §4). Accordingly, Islam is not considered by the Catholic Church to be a revealed religion.

Nevertheless the words used in *Nostra Aetate* are significant, since they underline the importance of faith for Muslims. It is a faith that flows into life for, as *Nostra Aetate* says, "(Muslims) strive to submit themselves without reserve to the hidden decrees of God." This is the basic attitude of *islâm*, which is by no means a fatalistic submission to a despotic divinity but the response of an adoring servant (*'abd*) to a transcendent God who remains wrapped in mystery.

Paragraph 3 of *Nostra Aetate* thus mentions the fact of Muslims' belief in, and response to, a God who reveals, but it says nothing about the manner of this revelation. Just as Muhammad is not mentioned, neither is there any reference to the Qur'an. Yet Islam would claim to be "a religion of the Book," and the Qur'an plays a central role in Islamic worship and life. Moreover, Islam readily classifies Jews and Christians, together with Muslims, as "People of the Book." Christians may well object to this classification since they consider themselves to be followers of a person, Jesus Christ, and not of a book. Moreover, the notions of revelation and the role of the scriptures are not the same in the two religions. As has been said above, there is not the same relationship between Islam and Christianity as there is between Christianity and Judaism. Christianity accepts the Jewish Scriptures as part of its own revelation, but it does not accept Islam as a biblical religion. Moreover, from the side of Islam, the link between the Qur'an and the Christian Scriptures, including the Old Testament, is very tenuous. There are some references in the Qur'an to biblical elements, but the texts of the previous scriptures are not retained as such—in fact the criticism is leveled that they have been falsified—and they are certainly not used in Islamic worship.

Both texts of Vatican II link Islamic faith with Abraham. *Lumen Gentium* says that Muslims "profess to hold the faith of Abraham." *Nostra Aetate* states that Muslims submit to God "just as Abraham submitted himself to God's plan, to whose faith Muslims eagerly link their own." It must be admitted that these references *en passant* to Abraham remain somewhat vague. Abraham's faith is recognized, but it is not said how he exemplified this faith. Muslims see Abraham as a champion of monotheism and attribute to him the rebuilding of the Ka'ba, the shrine in Mecca in the direction of which Muslims turn in prayer. Christians insist on Abraham's response to God's call to leave his country for a promised land. By both religions, Abraham is given as a model of submission to God's mysterious decrees. This spirit of submission was illustrated in a preeminent way in his readiness to sacrifice his son, an episode in Abraham's life exalted by Jews, Christians, and Muslims, but with a different identification of the victim.

There is silence above all on the question of descent from Abraham. The first version of the text to be introduced into *Lumen Gentium*, following the line advocated by Massignon and his disciples, read: "The sons of Ishmael, who recognize Abraham as their father and believe in the God of Abraham, are not unconnected with the Revelation made to the patriarchs." The reference to Ishmael was removed. Quite apart from the historical question of the descent of the Arabs from Abraham through Ishmael, something that remains disputed, the silence on this point is quite consistent with the Christian position with regard to Abraham. As has been illustrated in the first section of this paper, the New Testament teaches that physical descent is unimportant; it is faith that counts. There are indeed profound differences in the way Jews, Christians, and Muslims see Abraham, yet there is a common recognition of Abraham as a model of faith and submission. As long as there is a readiness to respect the different interpretations, the figure of Abraham provides common ground for the followers of Judaism, Christianity, and Islam, which can be called with some justification "Abrahamic religions," though this term does not describe them adequately or completely.

Since Vatican II there has been very little change in the position of the church with regard to Islam. The *Catechism of the Catholic Church* is content to repeat the conciliar statements. In the teachings of the popes two ideas appear, which, if not completely new, strike a slightly different tone. The first of these is a reference to common bonds. John Paul II, addressing the Catholic community in Ankara, Turkey, in November 1979, appealed to them "to recognize and develop the spiritual bonds that unite us [i.e., Christians and Muslims]."[18] Similarly, in his discourse to young Muslims in Casablanca in August 1985, the pope stated: "The Catholic Church regards with respect and recognizes the quality of your religious progress, the richness of your spiritual traditions. I believe that we, Christians and Muslims, must recognize with joy the religious values that we have in common, and give thanks to God for them."[19] There is nothing grudging here. It is a call to spiritual emulation.

The second idea is that of brotherhood. Pope Paul VI, speaking to the Islamic communities of Uganda in 1969, had already expressed his hope "that what we hold in common may serve to unite Christians and Muslims more closely in true brotherhood."[20] John Paul II, meeting Muslims in the Philippines in 1981, laid even more emphasis on the same idea: "I deliberately *address you as brothers*: that is certainly what we are, because we are members of the same human family . . . but we are especially brothers in God, who created us and whom we are trying to reach, in our own ways, through faith, prayer and worship, through the keeping of his law and through submission to his designs."[21] It may seem as if this point is being belabored, but in the early church the term "brothers" was reserved for fellow Christians. The use of this term by the popes can be seen as a sign of openness and friendship, based on respect for the religion of Islam.

Bilateral, Trilateral, and Multilateral Relations

Vatican II encourages Catholics to engage in dialogue, in all prudence and charity, with people belonging to other religions, and this applies to Jews and Muslims in particular. The council does not lay down how this dialogue should be carried out. There are many different ways of developing the relations among the religions. It is perhaps well to treat separately bilateral, trilateral, and multilateral relations.

Bilateral relations, Jews–Christians and Christians–Muslims, are perhaps the most frequent, with specific Jewish–Muslim relations being less developed. Contacts can be official or unofficial, ongoing or sporadic. Here reference will be made to the more official structures of dialogue. Reference has been made above to the International Catholic–Jewish Liaison Committee. The International Council of Christians and Jews could also be mentioned. With regard to Muslims, the Catholic Church, through the Pontifical Council for Interreligious Dialogue, has established in recent years two committees. The Islamic–Catholic Liaison Committee brings Catholics together with representatives of international Islamic organizations. Alongside this there is the Joint Committee of the Pontifical Council and the Permanent Committee of Al-Azhar for Dialogue with Monotheistic Religions. Both of these committees meet annually and provide a forum for exchange on matters of common concern. There are also relations between the Pontifical Council and organs of particular Muslim majority countries, Iran, Libya, and Turkey, for example, and these give rise to regular colloquia. Mention should be made, too, of groups of Catholics and Muslims that meet regularly. In the United States there are three such groups that have been discussing issues together. On the Atlantic coast a group has been looking at the question of marriage and the family. In the Midwest the theme tackled was that of revelation, while in California attention focused on spiritual matters. Bilateral dialogue is a more suitable structure for examining theological questions, where attention is given to understanding the differences as well as looking for commonalities.

Trilateral dialogue, bringing together Jews, Christians, and Muslims, also exists, though not without difficulties, given the political situation in the Middle East. It is a recognition of the special bonds that unite the Abrahamic religions. In France, the *Fraternité d'Abraham* has been in existence for around fifty years. More recently another movement, *Les Enfants d'Abraham*, has been founded. The International Council of Christians and Jews has opened up some of its activities to Muslims. A move was made to make this body trilateral, but the suggestion was not accepted. This gave rise in the United Kingdom to the founding of the Three Faiths Forum. Trilateral dialogue would seem particularly appropriate for exploring spiritual themes, but it can also bring Jews, Christians, and Muslims to reflect on their common contribution to contemporary society.

Multilateral dialogue brings Jews, Christians, and Muslims into formal contact with people of other religions. Numerous multireligious movements exist, such as the Temple of Understanding, the World Conference of Religions for Peace, the United Religions Initiative, and many others. There are also local bodies, such as interreligious councils, in certain cities. As long as these bodies respect the identity of each religion and do not fall into syncretism, they can do much to create a spirit of understanding and cooperation among citizens belonging to different religions.

In trilateral and multilateral dialogue, some of the sharp focus of bilateral exchanges may be lost, but the enlargement of the forum of exchange may soften the asperity that can sometimes exist between people of two religions and may prevent the dialogue from becoming merely an exercise in polemics. There is surely a place for all three types of dialogue.

The Example of Abraham

One of the texts of the Qur'an about Abraham reads: "And (remember) when his Lord tried Abraham with (his) commands, and he fulfilled them. He said: Lo! I have appointed thee a leader for mankind" (Q 2:124). The Arabic word translated here as "leader" is *imam*. The same term is used in Islam for the person who leads the ritual prayer and thus stands before the people. The word, however, also means "model," and in this sense Abraham is given as an example for all human beings. In concluding this paper it may be appropriate to point out three ways in which Abraham can serve as a model today.

Having heard God's call, Abraham left his own country and set out into the unknown. In so doing he distanced himself from the polytheistic milieu in which he was living in order to obey God. This is surely something that believers are called to do today. There is a need to recover the sense of God. It is not a question of making a common front against secularism, since respect for the autonomy of the civil and religious spheres can bring advantages to society. It is rather a question of making sure that all reference to God not be excluded from public life, that the life of faith not be confined to the private domain. Moreover true faith in the one God implies the struggle against any form of *shirk,* that is, of associating something with God.[22] We are well aware that such association can take different forms in modern life (the search for power, the accumulation of wealth, etc.). A further implication is that faith in God, and faith in human beings who have been created in the image of God, can lead to healthy and positive criticism of civil authority. There is a need to struggle so that human dignity may be respected. This is a task that Jews, Christians, and Muslims can tackle together.

The text of *Nostra Aetate* refers to Abraham as the one who "submitted himself to God's plan." Abraham's readiness to sacrifice his son was a sign of this spirit of submission. Whatever the identity of the son to be sacrificed—and on this there is a difference of opinion between Jews and Christians, on the one hand, and Muslims on the other—Abraham, the father, must have suffered. Yet he did not lose his trust in God. Faced with suffering and the mystery of evil, whether physical or moral, we should not lose confidence. Nor is suffering to be avoided at all cost, as would seem to be the idea of many in society today. Of course, everything has to be done to alleviate suffering, but while always maintaining the trust that God is present in the midst of suffering and that God is the one who will conquer evil. It would be helpful to encourage our contemporaries to be more like Abraham, acting with force and perseverance but also with great humility, conscious that only God can give perfection.

Finally, there is the quality of friendship. Precisely because Abraham seeks to submit to God's will, he becomes God's friend (*khalil*). This friendship is not lived by Abraham in a self-centered way, cutting himself off from others. On the contrary, Abraham is impelled by his trusting friendship with God to intercede for those who are in need. There is a danger today of considering relationship with God as a strictly personal matter. We are faced with the "me" culture, even in the spiritual realm. What is important is *my* relationship with God, the building up of *my* religious personality, the attainment of *my* happiness. Abraham stands in stark contrast to this attitude. He gives the example of someone who is open to the needs of his brothers and sisters. In my opinion, this same openness is demanded of all the children of Abraham. It is good that we should rediscover ourselves as being members of the Abrahamic family, but this should not confine us within a closed circle. Our relationship with God, the God of Abraham, but also the God of the whole of humankind, should instill in us a spirit of compassion for our fellow human beings. Such an attitude can be expressed in prayer, bringing our brothers and sisters before God and imploring for them the divine blessing. It may be fulfilled by common action on behalf of our brothers and sisters whatever race or religion they may belong to. For the blessing bestowed on Abraham is a blessing for the whole world.

Notes

1. This view did not go uncontested in the early church, as attested by the heresy of Marcion (d. ca. 160), who accepted as authentic scripture only ten letters of Paul and an edited version of the Gospel of Luke.

2. *Catechism of the Catholic Church* (2nd ed.; Strathfield, NSW: St. Paul's Publications, 2000) (henceforth abbreviated *CCC*; the numbers refer to paragraphs).

3. The *Catechism* goes on to state in a later section that "against all human hope, God promises descendants to Abraham, as the fruit of faith and of the power of the Holy Spirit. In Abraham's progeny all the nations of the earth shall be blessed. This progeny will be Christ himself" (*CCC* §706). The final phrase is rather abrupt, introducing as it does the specific Christian understanding of the promise made to Abraham. This is based on Paul's letter to the Galatians: "Now the promises were addressed to Abraham and to his descendant"—notice that scripture does not use a plural word as if there were several descendants; it uses the singular: "to his posterity, which is Christ" (Gal. 3:16). Paul's conformity with the tradition he received could be confirmed here by a reference to the first line of the Gospel of Matthew: "A genealogy of Jesus Christ, son of David, son of Abraham" (1:1).

4. Benedict T. Viviano, "The Gospel According to Matthew," in *The New Jerome Biblical Commentary*, ed. Raymond E. Brown, Joseph A. Fitzmyer, and Roland E. Murphy (London: Geoffrey Chapman, 1990), 637.

5. This document was published by the newly established Commission for Religious Relations with Jews (CRRJ). In 1966 an Office for Catholic–Jewish Relations had been created within the Secretariat for Promoting Christian Unity that had carried this concern from the time of the preparation of the Second Vatican Council. Pope Paul VI, in 1974, decided on the establishment of the CRRJ as a distinct organ but still connected to the Pontifical Council for Promoting Christian Unity. In the meantime, in 1970, the International Jewish Committee on Interreligious Consultations (IJCIC) had come into existence. In the same year a Memorandum of Understanding was agreed upon between IJCIC and various officials of the Roman Curia to set up the International Catholic–Jewish Liaison Committee.

6. Some manuscripts, however, read the singular, *diathēkē*, which would refer only to the covenant of Sinai; see Joseph A. Fitzmyer, "The Letter to the Romans," in *New Jerome Biblical Commentary*, ed. Brown et al., 856.

7. The capital letters indicate perhaps a greater degree of importance.

8. Norbert Lohfink, *The Covenant Never Revoked* (New York/Mahwah, N.J., Paulist Press, 1991), 9.

9. Ibid., 83.

10. Ibid., 85.

11. Eugene J. Fisher, "Pope John Paul II's Pilgrimage of Reconciliation: A Commentary on the Texts," in Eugene J. Fisher and Leon Klenicki, *John Paul II on Jews and Judaism 1979-1986* (Washington D.C.: United States Catholic Conference, 1987), 13.

12. The Pontifical Council for Promoting Christian Unity, *Information Service*, 112 (2003/1): 35.

13. Pontifical Council for Interreligious Dialogue, Congregation for the Evangelization of Peoples, *Dialogue and Proclamation* (Vatican City, 1991), nos. 40-41. The quotation within the text is from a previous document: Secretariat for Non Christians, *The Attitude of the Church toward the Followers of Other Religions* (Vatican City, 1984), no. 37. The text also bears a reference to *Dignitatis Humanae* no. 2.

14. Pontifical Council for Promoting Christian Unity, *Information Service* 111 (2002/4): 236-37.

15. For what follows, further details and references will be found in Michael L. Fitzgerald, "From Heresy to Religion: Vatican II and Islam," in *Europe and Islam: Evaluations and Perspectives at the Dawn of the Third Millennium*, ed. Mahmud Salem Alsheikh (Florence: Florence University Press, 2002), 53-71.

16. Judaism, Christianity, and Islam are often referred to as "the three monotheistic religions." That they are monotheistic religions is true, and the texts of Vatican II can be seen to bear witness to this fact. Yet to talk about *the three* monotheistic religions would seem to be an exaggeration. There are in fact other monotheistic religions. One has only to think of the Sikhs. If the three religions of Judaism, Christianity, and Islam are to be brought together in a special way, another category has to be found.

17. Robert Caspar, "Islam According to Vatican II," in *Signs of Dialogue*, ed. Michael L. Fitzgerald and Robert Caspar (Zamboanga City: Silsilah Publications, 1992), 240.

18. See Francesco Gioia, *Interreligious Dialogue: The Official Teaching of the Catholic Church* (Boston: Pauline Books & Media, 1997), no. 339.

19. See ibid., no. 474.

20. See ibid., no. 263.

21. See ibid., no. 363 (emphasis in original).

22. *Shirk* refers to something that is not God that can take the place of God: for instance, a finite object of love or concern that becomes all-consuming and thereby threatens the oneness of God and risks being an idol. The Christian analogue can be found in Augustine's treatment of a disordered love, in which one puts something before God as the supreme good, or when Paul Tillich writes of a finite concern that becomes an ultimate concern.—Eds.

Relations among the Abrahamic Religions: RESPONSE

Reuven Firestone

ARCHBISHOP MICHAEL FITZGERALD offers a noteworthy account of some of the important theological issues separating Roman Catholic Christianity, Judaism, and Islam. Even in this short paper, he has taught me a great deal, and I am thankful for the opportunity to learn from his knowledge and wisdom. As I read his words and the words of the scriptures, liturgy, catechism, and papal commissions that the archbishop cites, I found myself becoming a bit agitated, realizing that two words kept creeping into my mind: "humility" and "pride." I was moved by the archbishop's deep humility, while at the same time distressed by the pride that seems to inform the positions he represents. I wish to stress that I respect the tremendous steps that the church has taken, continuing to this day, with the Second Vatican Council's declaration *Nostra Aetate*. But I also observed a language of dichotomies and of theological certainty that I find problematic, not only in situations of religious dialogue but simply in theological discourse in general. My critique is not a critique of the church, per se; rather, it is a critique of the language of theological dogma.

How is one to know, for example, that "Abraham's hope, based on faith, included faith in the resurrection . . . that God could bring life from what was practically a dead body"? In the discourse of Jewish study we would ask, "How do we know this?" And we would then search the available record of the divine will in order to collect a range of possible answers. As a Jew I would normally limit my first examination to the Jewish scriptural canon, and I would find no indication that Abraham's hope included faith in the resurrection. In fact, there is no clear statement of belief in resurrection throughout the Hebrew Scriptures until one comes to chapter 12 of the book of Daniel.[1]

In an interreligious context I seek understanding also from Christian Scripture, and as Archbishop Fitzgerald notes, Hebrews 11 provides authoritative support for Abraham's believing in the resurrection of the dead. But this is a Christian gloss, which uses the Hebrew Bible as an authenticating tool to justify a non-Hebrew biblical concept.

I do not find this process of interpretation problematic, because scripture is always engaged in a kind of dialogue, not only with humanity but also with itself. From my Jewish perspective, it is arbitrary to consider the New Testament's relationship with the Hebrew Bible one of culmination or proof of certain specific constructs found in the earlier scripture while ignoring many others. Paul's divinely grounded interpretation of Genesis needs to be seen, rather, as part of a larger "scriptural dialogue." Why can't it be said that the newer revelation of the Christian Bible made the concept of resurrection, which was only emerging in the two centuries leading up to it, authoritative and acceptable to a community of believers? Why insinuate that characters of the Hebrew Bible also believed this? When this is communicated, it suggests that Jews today who do not believe in Christian theologies introduced as glosses on Hebrew Bible texts are errant. It suggests that Jews are not true even to their own scripture.

We are confronted with the persistent problem in dialogue of rival or competing scriptures. This is an extremely difficult problem between the scriptural Abrahamic religions because each of our scriptures is understood to announce that it is the last word in scriptural prophecy. The relationships and attitudes toward other scriptures among the three families of religion are complex and far beyond the scope of this discussion, but I was struck by Archbishop Fitzgerald's comment that "Jews and Christians do not accept the Qur'an as revelation from God. If they did, they would become Muslims."

I wonder why I must necessarily become a Muslim if I accept the Qur'an as a revelation from God, or Christian if I accept the Christian Bible in the same way? Can I, as a Jew, accept the Hebrew Bible as a revelation but not the only revelation? Can I, as a Jew, understand the Christian Bible and the Qur'an as divine revelations that were, simply, not directed to me? According to dogmatic positions found in all three systems, it seems, accepting the possibility of another revelation is axiomatically considered to be the invalidation of commitment to one's own traditional revelation. But why is this conclusion necessary? Must I believe every part of the Christian Bible or the Qur'an in order to consider it divine revelation? Must I believe in the absolute truth and immutability of every part of these texts?

When one reads any single scripture, let alone compares two or more, one cannot help but note that God is engaging in dialogue with humanity. God speaks in many ways—through commandments, parables, homilies, poetry, and narrative stories—because humans arrive at understanding in a variety of ways and with a range of personal conclusions. There seem to be very few cases in which scripture communicates theological points in an absolutely clear and consistent manner. Most often, scriptural discourse tends to be obscure, even ambiguous, and it allows for and even seems to encourage a range of personal understanding.

From their earliest commentaries on scripture, theologians and religious scholars have operated with confidence in the belief that this ambiguity is a product of God's wisdom, for had God desired clarity, there would be clarity. The lack of transparency therefore must be intentional. The result has been, from our earliest record of scriptural interpretation to this day, a range of human understandings that are derived from our personal responses to the scriptural records of the divine will. The variety of scriptural discourse and its dialogical nature naturally stimulate the God-given inclination of humanity to think creatively. Dogmatic discourse discourages or forbids such a natural, human response to scripture, and it is the dogmatic inclination in any religion that I find problematic.

Archbishop Fitzgerald offers some traditional Catholic teachings that are contrary—even objectionable—to the sensibilities of Jews or the various positions of Rabbinic Judaism. One teaches that the ultimate meaning of Abraham is in his role as progenitor of Jesus, another that the church's mission of salvation is mystically prefigured in the exodus. Although these conclusions are unacceptable to Jews, it is important for Jews to think about them and understand that they are sources of deep meaning for Catholics. In the dialogic process, it is the consideration of ideas rather than the proclamation of doctrine that leads to better understanding across boundaries and a greater likelihood for mutual respect. The archbishop has demonstrated how the Holy See has moved in this direction in his citation of the Pontifical Council for Interreligious Dialogue's *Dialogue and Proclamation*.

This document notes that through engagement in interreligious dialogue, "'the decision may be made to leave one's own previous spiritual or religious situation in order to direct oneself toward another.' Sincere dialogue implies, on the one hand, mutual acceptance of differences, or even of contradictions, and on the other, respect for the free decision of persons made according to the dictates of their conscience (cf. *Dignitatis Humanae* §2)." As I read this, my first reaction was to wonder how the Catholic Church is able to accept the possibility that a Catholic engaging in dialogue with a Jew might wish to leave the church for Judaism. Does the recognition of the possibility of conversion go "both ways?" But I soon realized the answer is clearly yes, if indeed "the plan of salvation also includes [all] those who acknowledge the Creator."

After acknowledging my own defensiveness to some of Archbishop Fitzgerald's remarks, my thoughts turned to my own experience with interreligious dialogue. The truth of the matter is that I sometimes feel frustrated and defensive in dialogue. But rather than tempting me away from my own faith, my conversations with faithful Christian and Muslim religionists deepen my own commitment to Judaism because they broaden my understanding of the religious quest and increase my respect for the dignity of other religious paths.

For me, the most reassuring statement of Archbishop Fitzgerald's essay is this: "This does not mean that Jews in order to be saved have to become Christians; if they follow their own conscience and believe in God's promises as they understand them in their religious tradition they are in line with God's plan, which for us comes to its historical completion in Jesus Christ." For me, the key words here are "for us." When I read this, I scratched my own words in the margin: "Yes! 'For us,' but not for everyone."

That statement, "For us," reminded me of a theological conundrum that Jews had to confront in the Islamic world. Jews under Islam were occasionally subjected by local leaders to religious persecution and forced conversion, though this is forbidden according to Islamic law. A great medieval rabbi was asked whether it is acceptable for a Jew, under duress, to pronounce the *shahada*, the ultimate statement of faith for Islam and the formal statement of conversion: "There exists no god aside from [the one great] God, and Muhammad is prophet of God." All Jews could proclaim the first part of the statement, for believing Jews, by definition, believe in the singular God of the universe. A problem arises only with regard to the second part of the creedal statement. In the Arabic as well as its English translation, the second part has some ambiguity, for it does not say that Muhammad is God's greatest prophet or even last prophet. Neither does it claim that Muhammad is God's prophet for all peoples. Could it not be possible for a Jew to acknowledge that Muhammad is a true prophet, but a prophet for the Muslims and not for the Jews? The rabbi, noting the ambiguity, answered in the affirmative. A Jew could pronounce the *shahada*, "There exists no god aside from God, and Muhammad is prophet of God," but with the quiet addition of one very small Hebrew word, "*lahem*"—"for them."

Note

1. Ezekiel's 'dry bones' is almost certainly a metaphor for the renewal of the people of Israel. It does happen that resurrection of the dead becomes a generally accepted belief in Rabbinic Judaism, but this is developed in the Jewish equivalent of the new Christian Scripture, the Jewish "Oral Torah" or Talmud (see Mishnah Sanhedrin, ch. 10).

Relations among the Abrahamic Religions: Response

Mahmoud M. Ayoub

ARCHBISHOP FITZGERALD'S ESSAY is a rich contribution to interfaith dialogue among the followers of the Abrahamic faith traditions. His starting point is the well-known rule *lex orandi, lex credendi*. While this focus allows him to explore the close relationship between faith and theology in the Catholic tradition, it imposes a degree of rigidity on his presentation, which inadvertently gives a tone of over-self-confidence to his argument. Nonetheless, Archbishop Fitzgerald's courage, honesty, and commitment to his own faith and to interreligious ecumenism are clearly discernible throughout his essay.

Archbishop Fitzgerald begins by applying his rule to the offerings of the Mass, or Eucharistic Prayer, where God is asked to accept the offerings of the celebrants as he did the offerings of Abel, Abraham, and Melchizedek. In his anxiety to show the continuity of these ancient offerings to God with the death and resurrection of Christ, Archbishop Fitzgerald overlooks the fact that Melchizedek, whose blessing Abraham sought, was not of the line of prophets or priests from Abraham to David; he was a Canaanite priest. This raises the question, at least in the mind of a non-Christian believer in God's universal love and providence, could not this righteous Gentile priest represent the non-Hebrew people of God, including the Arabian prophet? Unless and until we can see God's workings in all three monotheistic religions, meaningful dialogue among God's children is no more than a social formality. Christians, of course, have every right to believe in the validity of this prayer for their faith and worldview, but should these ancient covenants allow no other interpretation?

Another important point is the continuity between the image of Abraham in the Christian and Islamic traditions. For us all, he is "our father in faith." He is the model of true obedience (*islam*) to God. He is also the model of absolute trust in God. He accepted all of God's commands without question or hesitation, because he knew that God would not betray his intimate friend. It was, according to the Qur'an, after Abraham fulfilled all God's commands, that God made him an *imam*, or leader for humankind (Q 2:124). Traditionally, an *imam* is a source of blessing for his followers. Hence, Abraham is a source of blessing for all of humanity, not through his progeny but in himself. These important common points are obscured by the theology of the cross of Christ, which dominates Archbishop Fitzgerald's discussion.

Although I should perhaps concentrate on what Archbishop Fitzgerald says about Catholic–Muslim relations, his treatment of Jewish–Catholic relations calls for some comments. Relying on the Vatican II historic document *Nostra Aetate*, Archbishop Fitzgerald tries at one and the same time to include Judaism and the Jews in the divine economy of salvation and to exclude them. Among the different Christian interpretations of the "old and new covenants," he prefers, I think, the "one covenant theory," which asserts the unity of the first and second covenants, that is, the covenant to the prophets and patriarchs of ancient Israel and the covenant through Christ with all of humanity. Yet the church has always upheld the principle that the "old covenant," with all its affirmations and renewals, was fulfilled and superseded by Christ. How can both covenants then be equally valid?

I see two problems in this position. The first is that the New Testament and subsequent Christian theology have insisted on the fact that the law and rituals of the ancient Hebrews, as recorded in the Bible and developed by later tradition, have been abrogated by the life, death, and resurrection of Christ. Therefore, to acknowledge the truth of Judaism and still continue to witness for Christ to the Jews is a contradiction in terms, which, to say the least, is untenable.

The second problem is the clear difference between the positive and apologetic attitude toward the Jews and Judaism, on the one hand, and the condescendingly tolerant attitude toward Muslims and the dismissive attitude toward Islam, on the other. I will have more to say about this point later. The question for me is why the "one covenant" cannot include Islam and Muslims. Perhaps part of the reason is that the church has for some time now been trying to justify itself to the Jews, to claim for itself a place in the old covenant, which it can no longer claim as its exclusive property. With regard to Islam, the church has so far failed to find room in God's plan of salvation for a post-Christian religion. I believe that the only way out of this theological dilemma is for all of us to adopt a multicovenant theory, that is, a special covenant with each of the Abrahamic communities and one universal divine covenant with all of humanity. In fact, we need to develop a theology of a plurality of covenants between God and all religious communities and individuals that accept faith in God and hope in God's mercy.

The section dealing with the relations of the Catholic Church with Islam and Muslims begins with the usual contrast of attitudes of each of the three faith communities toward one another: the Jews do not accept the New Testament as the word of God, for if they did, they would be Christians; Muslims acknowledge that both the Torah and the gospel were revealed by God, but neither the Jews nor Christians acknowledge the Qur'an as a divine revelation.

I am sure that Archbishop Fitzgerald knows that the assertion of the strictly divine origin of the New Testament is a later Protestant idea. The New Testament is part of the living tradition of the Christian Church. The church appropriated the Hebrew Bible particularly after the first generations of Jewish Christians and made it part of its own heritage, but denied its Jewish meaning and validity.

Let me return to the issue at hand. Were the Jews and Christians to accept the Qur'an as a divine revelation, Archbishop Fitzgerald argues, "they would become Muslims." On this point, Jews, Christians, and Muslims have, in my view, violated the principle of the infinite mercy of God to which their traditions testify. The Muslims have contradicted the spirit of the Qur'an, which calls on Jews, Christians, and Muslims to accept each other's scriptures as divine revelations and to acknowledge that they all profess faith in the one God. They did so by insisting that Islam has abrogated all previous religions and that the Qur'an has abrogated all scriptures. Some Jews have accepted the validity of Islam and the prophethood of Muhammad, but only for the Arabs. More generally, they denied any claim to prophethood outside their own biblical history. However generous Christians may have been, they have so far rejected both Muhammad and the Qur'an. They have only acknowledged Muslims as good people of faith who, like them, "adore the one Merciful God." But even this somewhat positive assertion has been questioned by some Christian theologians on the grounds that Muslims do not accept Jesus as God. As for the Muslim side, the Qur'an enters into direct theological dialogue with Christians. Even though it rejects the doctrine of the Trinity, in whatever form it may be formulated, it does not question Christians' monotheistic faith. It regards Christology as a manifestation not of rejection of faith but of theological extremism (Q 4:171).

Long before Vatican II, and specifically *Lumen Gentium*, the Qur'an affirmed, "We do not worship different divinities, since God is one." Thus, both the Qur'an and subsequent Islamic tradition distinguish between religions that are based on revealed scriptures and those that are based on human wisdom or local myths and legends. The first are called "heavenly religions," and the second are often misrepresented as "idolatrous religions." In my view, all religions are ways to God. What distinguishes the Abrahamic traditions is their faith in a God who is active in human history, a God who reveals his will to his human creatures. He is not only the God of Abraham, Isaac, and Jacob, but of Ishmael as well.

Archbishop Fitzgerald rightly observes that all Vatican II documents referring to Islam speak not of Muhammad and the Qur'an but only of Muslims. This is also generally true of papal statements since Vatican II. I have argued, both in my essay and in my reply to Archbishop Fitzgerald's response to it, that neither the Qur'an nor the Prophet Muhammad expected any more of Christians and Jews than their recognition of the authenticity of the Qur'an as a divine revelation and of Muhammad as a messenger sent by God. The Muslims wrongly equated such recognition with conversion to Islam and the Christians equated it with denying the completeness and finality of the mission of Christ. I believe that neither of the two positions is conducive to meaningful dialogue.

I generally agree with Archbishop Fitzgerald's recommendations for dialogue and with his assessment of the bilateral and trilateral relations among the followers of the Abrahamic traditions. My only reservations are regarding the statements of His Holiness Pope John Paul II. I believe that the pope negated his positive statements by his discussion of Islam in his book *Crossing the Threshold of Hope*, published in 1994. In this book he denies that Muslims have a proper understanding of God. He has not always been consistent, telling Muslims that we are brothers, worshiping the One God, but at the same time urging Christians to preach to Muslims with the view to possible baptism. I believe that honest and constructive dialogue must take place among honest equals, women and men who seek not to make more Christians or Muslims but to understand and do the will of God.

Relations among the Abrahamic Religions: Reply

Michael L. Fitzgerald

BOTH PROFESSOR FIRESTONE and Professor Ayoub have managed to pack many acute observations into the few pages of their responses. Before responding to some of their remarks I wish to make a general observation.

Following Wilfred Cantwell Smith, a number of scholars have suggested that we should be moving toward a world theology. They feel that the language used in theological reflection must be acceptable to all readers, to whatever religion they belong. Yet this would seem to be a rather futile endeavor. An attempt is made to suit everybody, but the end result satisfies no one. Theology, by its very nature, implies a reflection on reality from a particular standpoint; if it is Christian theology, this means in the light of the scriptures as received through the tradition of the church. If one would wish to move to another standpoint, what would be the criterion for the choice of this particular standpoint rather than another? Consequently the statements made in Christian theology do not have to be acceptable to the followers of another religious tradition, in this case to my Jewish and Muslim brothers and sisters. What can be hoped for is not agreement, or at least not more than partial agreement, but certainly a clearer understanding of our positions. This clarity is important since it helps us to know where we stand, and this in turn can help us to live and work together, despite our differences. If such a position is considered arrogant, all I can say is that this is not intended. As Professor Firestone remarks, it is the consideration of ideas in a dialogic process that leads to better understanding.

Professor Firestone, referring to the meditation on Abraham in the Letter to the Hebrews, does not consider the Christian gloss problematic, but does feel that there is an implied rejection of the Jewish understanding of the same passage as being invalid. I am sure that no Catholic exegete would hold this. Yet there are different levels of meaning. The texts of the First Testament are to be understood first of all in their historic context, but they are also seen in the light of the experience of Christ. Persons and events are reinterpreted in this light. Obviously such meanings cannot be imposed on people who do not share the same standpoint. No criticism is implied of those who do not see things in the same way.

Again Professor Firestone finds a problem if each Abrahamic religion sees its scripture as "the last word in prophecy." As far as the Christian understanding of scripture is concerned, a distinction would have to be made. Yes, it is the last word in the sense that nothing further essential for salvation remains to be revealed. No, it is not the last word, since there is the possibility of God giving a reminder through someone, recalling things that may have been forgotten, or announcing things that are to come. According to Catholic teaching, revelation is complete with the death of the last apostle, but the church recognizes the charism of prophecy announcing God's word in a particular place at a particular time, with a message for a particular person or a group of persons. An example is to be found in the book of Acts. A prophet called Agabus foretells that Paul is to be taken prisoner in Jerusalem and handed over to the Romans (see Acts 21:10-11). It must be remembered too that scripture is not static. Inspired by the Spirit, it is a living text capable of producing fruit at different times and in different circumstances. As Professor Firestone notes, the very ambiguity or mysteriousness of the scriptural texts allows God to speak through them at a particular point in life.

Nevertheless, this does not conflict with dogma, the clear expression of belief, whose role is not to obstruct the understanding of faith but rather to channel it into a more fruitful direction.

Professor Ayoub also has interesting questions about the interpretation of scripture. He seems to think, erroneously, that I take Melchizedek as a Hebrew priest of the line of Aaron (not Abraham as he says) and asks whether this Canaanite priest-king "could not represent non-Hebrew people, including the Arabian prophet?" There could surely be no objection to this interpretation, since the Catholic teaching on the Eucharist is that the offering of Christ subsumes all other offerings.

Something similar can be said about the covenants: the earlier covenants are subsumed in the New Covenant in Christ. It is important to note that they are not abrogated, as Professor Ayoub would seem to believe. The *Catechism* of the Roman Catholic Church, much used in my paper, can be referred to yet again. It states: "The covenant with Noah remains in force during the times of the Gentiles, until the universal proclamation of the Gospel" (*CCC* §58). I think no Catholic would maintain that the gospel has been preached everywhere, certainly not adequately, and therefore for many this covenant of Noah can remain in force.

Nevertheless this affirmation has to be understood in the light of the history of salvation, which, for Christians, is centered on Christ. It is Christ's passion, death, and resurrection that are the true way to salvation, but the Second Vatican Council teaches that the Holy Spirit gives all people, in ways known to God, the possibility of entering into this mystery (see *Gaudium et Spes* §22). The ways are known to God, but we can surmise that the rites and precepts of different religions, including those of Islam, make a contribution; they can lead people to die to themselves and live for others, which is, one could say, the essence of the paschal mystery.

This leads to the importance of mission for Christians, but mission understood as witness. Christians are called to announce what God has done in Jesus Christ and to announce this to all, including Jews and Muslims. Yet this is different from targeting Jews and Muslims. It means being ready to share one's belief, precisely because it is held to be precious, and welcoming those who are attracted by that belief. All this is to be done in a dialogical way and with the maximum respect for the freedom of the other. This is why, it seems to me, there is no contradiction in Christians addressing Muslims as brothers (and sisters), as Pope John Paul II has done, while at the same time wishing to share with them the Christian faith and being ready to welcome them, through baptism, into the Christian community if this is the way the Spirit is leading them.

A further clarification needs to be made regarding the Catholic understanding of scripture. Professor Ayoub says that I must certainly be aware that "the assertion of the strictly divine origin of the New Testament is a later Protestant idea." He goes on to point out correctly that the New Testament is part of the living tradition of the church. In fact something similar could be said of the First Testament. It was part of tradition before it was written down. The impression is given, however, that the fact of being part of tradition disqualifies the scriptures from being of divine origin. This is not so. The human authors of the sacred books made use of their own knowledge and their own literary talent, or lack of it, yet they were guided by God, so much so that the result is considered to be both the work of God and the work of humankind. This is the Catholic understanding of biblical inspiration.

This leads me finally to comment on Professor Ayoub's remark about the correct understanding of the Qur'an. He would seem to suggest that the Qur'anic text does not really deny the essential mysteries of Christ and his mission, namely, his divine sonship and the reality of his passion, death, and resurrection. This would not be the usual way the Qur'an is understood. It will be interesting to see whether Professor Ayoub's interpretation will prevail.

4

Abraham and His Children

A Muslim Perspective

MAHMOUD M. AYOUB

Millata abikum Ibrahim hua al-ladhi sammakum al-muslimin min qabl.

It is the *milla* of your father Abraham. He it was who called you Muslims before. (Q 22:78)

THIS BRIEF AND SOMEWHAT ENIGMATIC Qur'anic phrase defines well the Islamic view of Abraham. He is not simply the father of Muslims but also the founder of Islam. It was to his communal religion (*millah*) that Muhammad is believed to have been sent by God to call the people of Makkah, all the Arabs, and all of humankind. Abraham is therefore, for Muslims, the father of all the people of faith and the archetypal founder of true religion.

The Qur'an uses two words for religion. The first is *din*, which means religion, broadly speaking, or a religious system by which an individual or society lives. It is a moral and spiritual set of values according to which individual men and women will be judged on the day of judgment, called in the Qur'an *yaum al-din*, the day of *din* (Q 1:4; 82:17-18).

The other word, *millah*, is a difficult term to translate. It signifies religion not in the abstract sense, but the religion of a community.[1] The Qur'an says that Jews and Christians will not be pleased with Muhammad unless he enters into their *millah*, that is, adopts their religio-communal identity (Q 2:120). In other Islamic languages, as, for example, Persian, Turkish, and Urdu, the term *millah* took on the extended meaning of "nation," with or without reference to religion. Taking all these significations together, it may be concluded that *millah* means the religious polity of a distinct people or nation. Therefore, *millah* is best thought of as a community with a distinct religious identity.

I have dwelt at some length on the term *millah* because it defines both Islam and Muslims in relation to Abraham and, consequently, to the faith communities associated with him. For Muslims, Abraham, like all other prophets, is not just a pious individual but a prototype of the perfect human being as created by God before he/she becomes defined by her/his environment. This uncorrupted state of humanity in which all human beings are originally made is called in the Qur'an *fitrah*, "the pure creation" of God that cannot be altered (Q 30:30).

Abraham is a prophet and yet more than a prophet; he is the father of all true prophets and a universal exemplar of pure faith in the One God. Since, moreover, prophetic existence manifests God's original pure creation, it is the highest or best form of human existence; therefore, it is the ultimate goal of the human quest for perfection. As a prophet who supremely embodies this goal, Abraham has been a role model for Muslims to emulate.

Prophets in Islam represent one of the two foci of history. History, in fact, is the history of divine authority represented by the prophets and of temporal authority represented by kings. The first major Muslim historian, Muhammad b. Jarir al-Tabari (d. 923), titled his world history *The History of Prophets and Kings*.[2] Tabari's *History* begins not with the rise and fall of empires but with the lives of the patriarchs of ancient Israel, who were the first heroes of this prophetic history. Human history is in reality the instrument of

God's actions in the affairs of human societies, which ought to be regulated by the law of God as promulgated and executed by His prophets, and in the temporal history of particular nations, which is directed by kings. In the end, however, both authorities are mandated by God. God's wisdom and inscrutable will are manifested in the sad cycles of history—of the successive rise and fall of nations and empires—of which Surah 3 of the Qur'an reminds us: "Say, O God, Master of all dominion, You grant dominion to whomever You will, and You seize dominion from whomever You will, You exalt whomever You will and You abase whomever You will. . . ." and "Such are the days that We alternate among humankind."[3]

Generally, Muslims have been all too aware of the transience of human authority, however formidable it may be. They have been reticent, therefore, to acknowledge any authority as representing a real and everlasting power. They have likewise eschewed any absolute claim that any land is anyone's eternal homeland, country, or possession. The earth belongs to God alone, who had decreed that it be the inheritance of His righteous servants. In a rare instance where the Qur'an directly quotes the Hebrew Scriptures, it says: "And we have inscribed in the Psalms after the remembrance [of God], 'The earth shall surely be inherited by my faithful servants'" (Q 21:105).[4]

On the stage of world history, God asserts absolute dominion through the activities of His prophets, whose mission is to warn errant nations of God's impending punishment and call on them to mend their ways. When such nations stubbornly refuse to heed the warnings of their prophets, God's judgment falls upon them and they are destroyed. The great Muslim social historian and philosopher of history 'Abd al-Rahman Ibn Khaldun (d. 1406) bases his well-known theory of history on this Qur'anic worldview. For Ibn Khaldun, the nation is an organic body, much like the human individual. It is born, matures, declines, and dies, either through a natural catastrophe as punishment for its sins, or through conquest by another nation that succeeds it. Eventually, however, the conquering nation will itself suffer the same fate.[5]

Muslims, Christians, and Jews have shared this prophetic history and fought over who truly possesses it and particularly its great hero, Abraham.

Let us briefly look at what we, as children of Abraham, have shared and at what we have been fighting over. Then let us ponder the fundamental question: Who are the children of Abraham? This question is not an academic curiosity but a defining issue of our historical, theological, and, since the rise of modern Zionism and Arab nationalism, political relations. It has been both the cause of conflict and the basis of interfaith dialogue among the followers of the three Abrahamic faith traditions.

In Abraham we all share a father in both the physical sense and the metaphysical, or spiritual, sense. Abraham is believed to be the physical father of Arabs and Jews and, by extension, the moral and spiritual father of all Christians and Muslims as well.

In the fatherhood of Abraham we have the foundations of our common religious heritage, but also in this common paternity lie the roots of our historical religious and political conflicts. This is because each of our three faith communities wants our venerable patriarch for itself alone. As the Qur'anic verse with which I began these reflections clearly asserts, it was not Muhammad but Abraham who first called the Muslims *muslims*.

The Abrahamic Heritage: Shared and Contested

The exclusive claim of the Jews to Abraham is implicitly asserted in denying Abraham's firstborn, Ishmael, his rights of primogeniture. The name Ishmael (*yishma'el*) means "God hears," making Ishmael, too, a child of a divine promise, an answer to the prayer of his father Abraham. Furthermore, although the book of Genesis showers blessings on Ishmael and his descendants, still Ishmael remains the son of the slave woman, in contrast to Isaac, who is the son of the slave woman's mistress, the legitimate wife of her master, Abraham. Hence, from the point of view of Jewish tradition, the heritage, or legacy, of Abraham belongs not to all his children, but only to the progeny of Isaac, the true son of the promise. Yet, from the point of view of general Semitic culture, it is patrilineal rather than matrilineal descent that defines a person. This remains true, notwithstanding the fact that today a person is legally a Jew whose mother is Jewish.

Biblical culture as well as later Jewish tradition lay far greater emphasis on paternity than maternity, so that a man is known as so-and-so, son of his father so-and-so. This has been true also of Muslim tradition and of most traditional Eastern Christian cultures. Yet, when the Muslims came in contact with European Jews and Christians, they were contemptuously called "sons of Hagar." This negative epithet has survived to our own time in the book, *Hagarism*, written, perhaps half in jest, by two respectable European scholars.[6] Of course, the aim of this derisive identification was not to emphasize the Abrahamic fatherhood of the Muslims but their maternal inferiority as the descendants of a black Egyptian handmaid.

The Qur'an and subsequent Islamic tradition, however, have upheld the equal legitimacy of the two sons of Abraham and assigned to each a special role in the covenantal history of humankind. Significantly, the Qur'an does not name Abraham's sacrificial son [who in the Muslim tradition is identified as Ishmael— Eds.], because it regards both children of Abraham as sons of the promise. Isaac had the privilege of being the progenitor of all the prophets of ancient Israel, including Jesus and his mother, Mary, as well as Zechariah and his son John the Baptist. Ishmael, on the other hand, was favored with being, along with his father Abraham, the builder of the Ka'bah of Makkah, "the first house for humankind," as a place of worship of the One God (Q 3:96; 2:127). He was, as well, the father of the Arabian prophets who came after Abraham, including Muhammad.

The significance of all that we share and fight over in this sacred prophetic history lies in God's covenant with Abraham. When God chose Abraham for His covenant, Abraham was a fugitive, running from one place to another without homeland or family. This man, who belonged to no land or nation, was chosen by God to be a source of blessing for all lands and nations.

Although God promised Abraham descendants as innumerable as the stars of heaven (Gen. 15:5), each of the three families—Jews, Christians, and Muslims—belied the universality of this divine promise by limiting the promise to each of the three families to the exclusion of any other tribe or nation. The Christian tradition exclusively appropriated Abraham by exclusively appropriating his covenant with God, which they believe to have been fulfilled in Christ. Christians have therefore undermined the significance of Abraham's spiritual fatherhood of both Muslims and Jews.

The Abrahamic covenant, according to the Book of Genesis, was between a frightened and overwhelmed man and an all-powerful deity (Gen. 15:1-21). Abraham, we are told, fell into such a deep sleep that he was taken for dead. Then God sealed His covenant with this nearly dead and helpless man by manifesting His own majesty and might in the tongue of fire that consumed the sacrificial animals that signified this covenant.

In form, the Abrahamic covenant was both old and new. It was old in that it followed the well-known covenantal rituals of ancient Mesopotamian peoples with their local deities. It was new in that it was initiated by the Maker of the heavens and earth. However, regardless of its form, this ancient covenant continues to shape the modern history of Jews, Christians, and Muslims.

The Qur'an, which came after both the Hebrew Bible and Christian New Testament, often recasts biblical events and personalities to fit its own worldview. Thus, it transformed Abraham from the timid and precautionary patriarch of Genesis into a robust and dynamic man, a daring idol breaker. The Abraham of the Qur'an was not only a determined and strong man; he was also a mischievous youth. When he broke the idols of his people, he spared the chief one and, according to midrashic and later Islamic tradition, hanged the axe that he used to break them around the chief idol's neck. When the people discovered their smashed gods, they suspected "a youth called Abraham." He sarcastically answered, "Ask them, perhaps they would speak." They had humbly to admit that idols cannot speak, which allowed Abraham to retort, "Do you then worship instead of God that which can do you neither good nor harm, fie on you and on what you worship instead of God; do you not understand?" (Q 21:60-67).

Like all the great people of history, the Qur'anic Abraham is both a paradigm and a paradox. He is at once an earnest yet uncertain seeker for God in a shining star, the luminous moon, and blazing sun, and also a true man of faith in the One God who is "the creator of the heavens and earth" (Q 6:77-79). He is a questioning doubter and also an obedient submitter (*muslim*) to God.

The Qur'an uses the sacrificial covenant ritual of Genesis to demonstrate God's power to create life and death and Abraham's questioning faith. Abraham prayed, "My Lord, show me how you raised the dead." God answered, "What! Do you not have faith?" "Yes," he answered, "but in order that my heart may rest at ease" (Q 2:260).[7] God then ordered Abraham to cut up four birds and scatter their dismembered carcasses on four different hills, then call them to him, and they would hasten to him alive. In this way the Qur'an links the historical covenant with Abraham to the primordial covenant between humanity and God, which affirms God's absolute sovereignty over His creation.

In accordance with this primordial covenant, all the children of Adam acknowledged God's absolute Lordship in their affirmative answer to the question, "Am I not your Lord?" God then warned them not to say on the day of resurrection, "we were heedless of this [pledge]." He then promised to guide humanity out of its heedlessness into living faith in Him alone. God would affect this guidance through a long series of prophets, beginning with Adam and ending with Muhammad (Q 7:172; 2:39; 4:165).

Subsequent to this primordial divine covenant with Adam and his progeny, God made a covenant with every prophet to acknowledge the prophet that came before him and to announce the coming of the one to succeed him (Q 3:81).[8] Thus Abraham is succeeded by his sons Ishmael and Isaac, and they are succeeded by Jacob and his twelve sons, the patriarchs (*al-asbat*) whom the Qur'an regards as prophets. The patriarchs are followed by Moses and his brother

Aaron, and these by David and his son Solomon. Finally, Jesus announced the Messenger to come after him, "whose name is Ahmad," that is Muhammad (Q 61:6).[9] All these prophets are, according to the Qur'an, of one progeny, and all were favored by God (Q 3:33-34).

Abraham: The Father of Humanity

Let us now return to the question, Who are the children of Abraham? Was it only Isaac? Isaac and Ishmael? Or do we consider all the children that Abraham had with Hagar, Sarah, and a third wife who remained generally anonymous? If Abraham's anonymous children were to be taken to represent all the nations that were to be blessed by him (Gen. 12:3b),[10] then Abraham could be regarded as the spiritual father of all of humankind.

All Jews, Christians, and Muslims share Abraham's faith, a faith that made him unique among all the people of faith. The New Testament declares, "Abraham had true faith in God and that was accounted for him as righteousness" (Rom. 4:3). The Qur'an insists that the Prophet Muhammad came not to bring a new religion but to turn his fellow Arab descendants of Ishmael from the worship of idols back to the faith of their father Abraham.

Abraham is the initiator of the *hajj* pilgrimage, which is one of the five pillars of Islam. The *hajj* is a unique social and spiritual moment in the life of every Muslim who is able to make the journey. The *hajj* experience links the present moment of the lives of the pilgrims to sacred prophetic history. This is because the rites of the *hajj* are reenactments of the experiences of Abraham and his family.

As the pilgrims circumambulate the Ka'bah and stop to pray at Abraham's station (*maqam*), they walk in the footsteps of the intimate friend (*khalil*) of God. After they run between the two hills of al-Safa and al-Marwa in emulation of Hagar's frantic running up and down these two hills in search of water for her dying son, they too are refreshed by the same water of the sacred well of Zamzam that revived Ishmael. When they observe the rite of stoning (*rajm*) Satan as Abraham did when Satan came to tempt him away from obeying God's command to offer Isaac as a sacrifice, they learn from the first absolute submitter to the will of his Lord what true *islam* is. The *hajj* pilgrimage concludes with an animal sacrifice commemorating Abraham's unquestioning willingness to offer his beloved son as a sacrifice and God's ransoming the son with a "tremendous victim" (Q 37:107). We can clearly see in all this that Abraham is far more than simply a common ancestor we all share.

Like all the prophets before and after him, Abraham had to have a small following to lend him support during his life and disseminate his message after his death. Abraham's followers were the members of his family, that is, his children and his nephew Lot, who too was a prophet. A prophet must as well have identifiable enemies. Abraham's enemy was Nimrod, the arrogant and wicked king who thought himself to be God.[11]

After a heated debate in which Abraham utterly confounded Nimrod's false claim to divinity, Nimrod threw Abraham into a blazing fire but God miraculously turned the fire "into coolness and peace for Abraham" (Q 2:258; 21:69).[12] God punished Nimrod by sending against him a vast army of flies, one of which entered into his skull through his nostril and slowly gnawed at his brain until he died. The aim of this fantastic tale is to demonstrate that God can use one of His weakest creatures to abase the high and mighty and thus affirm His absolute power in His creation.

Many of the events and anecdotes comprising the stories of both the biblical and Qur'anic Abraham are similar, but substantially different in intent and significant details. Yet Abraham is as uniquely a prophet of Islam as he is uniquely the father of the Jews. The point at issue here is, can Abraham play both roles simultaneously and without conflict? I believe he can, but his children are so far unwilling to accept each other's claims to their common inheritance.

Both the tensions and the promise that have characterized these conflicting claims have arisen primarily from Jewish, Christian, and

Muslim differences over the priority and status of Abraham's two children, Ishmael and Isaac. According to the Hebrew Bible, Ishmael was expelled with his mother at the insistence of Sarah, his stepmother, who became jealous of Hagar the handmaid and her son. The Qur'an regards Ishmael as a prophet with a mission away from his father's house. Thus, it was not Sarah's jealousy but God who ordered Abraham to leave Ishmael and his mother in the precincts of the sacred house of Makkah. There Abraham prayed, "My Lord, I have brought some of my family to dwell in an uncultivable valley near your sacred house. Make, therefore, the hearts of many peoples incline toward them and provide them with diverse fruits; and send them a messenger from among themselves to teach them the book and wisdom" (Q 14:37). Thus, the Prophet Muhammad is said to have asserted his claim to this sacred inheritance in the words, "I am the answer to the prayer of my father Abraham."[13]

According to the Qur'an and Islamic tradition, Abraham did not abandon Ishmael. Rather, he visited him frequently, and together they were entrusted by God to build His house and purify it for those who were to use it as a house of prayer (Q 2:125). In contrast, Ishmael appears in the Bible with his family only once after his expulsion, when Abraham died and both Ishmael and Isaac came together to wash and bury their father (Gen. 25:8-9).

The Qur'an upholds the logic of its worldview regarding the universality of faith and the special status of the children of Israel as heirs to the "holy land" which God promised to their father Abraham. God showed Abraham all the kingdoms of the earth as the inheritance of all his progeny and ordered the children of his grandson Israel to "enter the holy land" that He had prescribed for them (Q 5:21; 6:75). Abraham is a universal personality, and his inheritance is likewise a universal inheritance. Therefore, Abraham's true heirs are those who live his life of righteousness, his obedience, and his total submission to the will of God.

As a man of "pure faith," faith that is not bound by institutionalized religion or even scriptures, Abraham transcends religion. The

Qur'an declares, "Abraham was neither a Jew nor a Christian, but a man of pure faith, a true *muslim*." He was a true *muslim* "before the Torah and Gospel were revealed" (Q 3:67; 3:65).

Let me say a word about the term *islam* as used in the Qur'an to refer to Abraham's faith. He is often called a *hanif*, which means one who turned away from the worship of idols to the worship of the one God. The *hanif* was in fact a true *muslim*, a man or woman of faith. The term was used in its plural form (*Hunafa'*) to refer to those Makkans, including Muhammad before his call to prophethood, who rejected the idol worship of their people and lived as *muslims* before Islam. The word *islam* and its derivatives are used in this broad sense to characterize all those who professed faith in the One God before the establishment of Islam as an institutionalized religion.

The Qur'an draws a clear distinction between legal Islam, or outward Islamic identity, and true submission to God. On this deeper level, *islam* becomes synonymous with inner faith (*iman*) in God. This inner living faith becomes synonymous with a life of righteousness (*ihsan*), wherein a person of faith "worships God as though she-he sees Him and if they do not see Him He sees them."[14]

Interfaith Dialogue among the Children of Abraham

It is clear from what has been said so far that Abraham occupies a central place in the faith and history of Jews, Christians, and Muslims. We each have our own Abraham. The Jews have Abraham as their father and source of blessing. Christians have Abraham as the faithful covenanter with God whose covenant the church inherited through the "new covenant" in Christ. The Muslims have Abraham also as their father and as guide to the worship of the One God. Thus we each are favored with our own version of Abraham. But instead of accepting him as an archetypal human being, who at one and the same time can enter the history of our faiths and transcend them, each of his three families has sought to monopolize him while insisting on his universal significance.

Now, given the rich Abrahamic heritage in which we all share, the question is, can Abraham serve as the focus of interfaith dialogue among all his children? The dialogue I have in mind is one whose ultimate aim is to share not only Abraham's life and personality but also Abraham's faith. I am convinced that Abraham can be central to the dialogue, but we must first depoliticize him and set him free from the shackles of our modern nationalistic and even religious ideas and ideologies. In order for us to achieve these goals, we must strive to live the life of Abraham, a life of obedience and unquestioning faith.

If we could all claim Abraham as our father and live his life, a creative and meaningful dialogue would be possible. The life that should be our goal is a life of humble faith that seeks to share through dialogue the total Abraham: the Abraham of the House of Jacob, the Abraham of the Christianity, and the Abraham of the Qur'an and Islamic tradition. If Abraham is truly the father of all of us, then all these aspects of his personality and faith should be our common heritage.

Abraham's multifaceted personality demands a multifaceted approach to dialogue. An important type of dialogue that the prophetic heritage of Abraham calls for is the "dialogue of life." It is a living dialogue among members of churches, synagogues, and mosques as they work together for the causes of social justice and world peace.

The aim of this type of dialogue is to seek fairness and to dare to speak collectively against war and senseless killing on our city streets and in our public schools. It is to strive for a better world for us and our children. These are values we all cherish and strive to live by. They are an essential part of our Abrahamic heritage and the foundations of what I am calling the "dialogue of life." This is the most widespread and most concrete form of dialogue. Unfortunately, many of us make of this dialogue of life a kind of social etiquette. Consequently, we often reduce it from a dialogue of action to a formal exchange of polite courtesies.

I wish in no way to belittle the importance of courteous relations among people of different faith traditions. On the level of day-to-day interrelations, courtesy ought to be a polite expression of understanding and compassion. It is therefore a necessary precondition for any kind of deeper dialogue.

For centuries our greed for power and domination made even common courtesy a difficult goal to attain. This is because Jews, Christians, and Muslims did not live as equal citizens of a multi-religious nation state, but as subjects of a Christian or Muslim empire. As most of us now live as citizens of independent nation states, it is neither the church nor the Muslim *ummah* that defines our rights and duties but rather the secular state in which we live. With the end of Western colonialism of the Muslim world during the first half of the last century, almost all Muslim states have adopted a parliamentary democratic European state system. By so doing, they have opted for a secular state model, a state inhabited by people of diverse religious traditions, sects, and denominations. Officially, at least, these states are obligated to grant all their citizens the same privileges, rights, and responsibilities. Therefore, I believe that the modern nation state, be it Jewish, Christian, or Muslim, need not clash with or threaten the integrity and universal character of the People Israel, the Christian Church, or the Muslim *ummah*. On the contrary, the modern concept of citizenship provides the best framework for peaceful coexistence and dialogue on whatever level it may happen.

A second type of dialogue is what I would like to call the "dialogue of belief and doctrine." It is the dialogue of academics, theologians, and intellectuals. Even if this type of dialogue risks becoming an abstract endeavor, it is necessary in that it allows us as scholars to study together our common heritage. This is best achieved by objectively examining our particular literatures and traditions, which have so often touched and enriched one another.

Let me briefly illustrate my point. Abraham Geiger, the nineteenth-century Jewish reformer, raised an important question in a book entitled *What Did Muhammad Take from Judaism*.[15] Geiger's question was a rhetorical one, because he himself assumed, as did until recently all Western scholars of Islam since the eighteenth century, that Islamic disciplines such as law, Qur'anic exegesis, and classical historiography actually came from Jewish halakic and midrashic sources. No one denies that Islam was influenced by Judaism and Christianity. Jewish influences are especially obvious in Islamic jurisprudence, and Eastern monastic Christian influences are clearly discernible in classical Sufi spirituality. But now we believe that much of the midrashic literature that Jews and Muslims share appeared after Islam. It was therefore the result of a creative interaction between the two traditions rather than one community simply borrowing from the other. Likewise, after significant initial Christian influences on Islamic spirituality, both Catholic and Orthodox mystical traditions were influenced by Sufi ideas and practices.

A third type of dialogue that we ought to cultivate is the "dialogue of faith." The dialogue of faith I am calling for is one whose ultimate aim is to create a fellowship of faith among the children of Abraham. Through this dialogue of faith, your faith as a Christian or a Jew would deepen my faith as a Muslim and my faith as a Muslim would nurture your faith as a Jew or a Christian. This requires that we engage in dialogue on the basis of how each of our traditions defines itself, and not on our own view of what the tradition of the other is, or ought to be. This implies that we must refrain from judging the truth or falsity of the scripture of the other by the criteria of our own scripture and theology.

Meaningful dialogue is not only possible; it is in fact a growing phenomenon in our world. Unfortunately, it has not yet gone far enough to make a real difference in our communal, national, and international relations. We are still, in my view, bound by our ancient and medieval norms and thus unable to engage in an authentic dialogue of faith and action between groups of equal partners.

Fundamental obstacles in the way of achieving constructive dialogue are the respective Jewish, Christian, and Muslim worldviews. The Jews are generally not interested in converting others to their faith. Muslims and Christians, in contrast, are still fighting over the salvation of souls through mission and *da'wah* activities.

Let me again illustrate my point. The Jewish community sees itself as God's chosen people. Hence, its biblical heritage is definitive, not only for Jews but for the universe. Therefore, they are not fundamentally concerned with the destiny of the Gentiles, that is, all other communities and nations. However, this exclusive attitude has, at least from the viewpoint of Rabbinic Judaism, been counterbalanced with a more positive view of the righteous people of other nations and their religions. Thus, Moses Maimonides, the great Jewish rabbi and Arab philosopher, says that Islam and Christianity are willed by God because through them God delivered the Torah to the nations.

There is no doubt that the Second Vatican Council ushered in a new era in Muslim–Christian dialogue. Furthermore, the work of the World Council of Churches has greatly broadened the horizons of international Christian–Muslim relations. Christians are now willing to accept Muslims as genuinely pious people of faith who, like them, believe in the One God. But as the important Vatican II document *Nostra Aetate* points out, Muslims do not accept Jesus as God. This will forever remain a dividing point, but it should not be an insurmountable problem. Although Christians have come to accept Muslims as genuinely religious people, they have not been able to accept Islam as an authentic religious tradition. This is because to accept Islam as a genuine faith would be to admit that Christianity is essentially incomplete and that Christ's salvific mission is neither final nor complete.

On the other side, Muslims are willing to accept Christianity essentially as a true and genuine faith, but they do not accept Christians as true representatives of their own faith-tradition. The Christianity that Muslims accept is not the Christianity of the Christian Church, but the Christianity of the Qur'an and early Muslim tradition. Qur'anic Christianity is interesting and should be studied on its own, but it cannot serve as the basis of Christian–Muslim dialogue.

One final obstacle in the way of constructive and useful dialogue is our seemingly irreconcilable views of the nature and ultimate purpose of revelation. For Jews and Muslims, the revealed word of God is a book, the Torah and the Qur'an. But the Jews reject the Qur'an as revelation, including the Qur'anic view of Abraham. On the other hand, while Muslims recognize both the Torah and the Bible as divine revelations, they generally believe that both scriptures have been corrupted and therefore have no authority.

In Christianity, the divine word is not a book but the man Jesus Christ. For Christians therefore, the Torah is authentic, but only as the "Old Testament," the covenant fulfilled in Christ. Hence the Torah of the Jews was abrogated by the Old and New Testaments. As for the Qur'an, it cannot be a divine revelation, because revelation ceased with Christ.

In spite of our differences, we all wish to listen to the divine word, as it speaks to us through our scriptures. But the divine word seems to speak in different and mutually exclusive languages to each of our faith communities. However, if God created us all, as we all believe, then God must love us all and wish to guide us to Him. If this is true, then I see no problem with Christians and Jews accepting Muhammad as a prophet and the Qur'an as divine revelation. Muslims should also accept the authenticity of the Jewish and Christian Scriptures.

In my view the Qur'an preaches a message of religious pluralism. I am therefore convinced that the Prophet Muhammad wanted no more from Christians and Jews than to accept the authenticity of the Qur'an as a divine revelation and to recognize him as a messenger sent by God. The Qur'an calls on all of us, Jews, Christians, and Muslims, to accept the authenticity of each other's scriptures and faith.

When we do that, we can meaningfully enter into a true dialogue of faith. Then we can listen to the voice of God speaking to us through our different traditions. This can be done only when we engage in dialogue as equal human beings concerned with the dignity of all the children of Adam. The Qur'an declares, "We [God] have indeed honored the children of Adam and carried them over land and sea, provided them with good and wholesome things, and preferred them over many of our creatures" (Q 17:70). This divine favor is expressed in Christianity in the humanity of Christ. The Book of Genesis refers to this human dignity in the assertion that God created Adam and Eve in his image. I therefore believe that humankind is both divine and human. There is much that we can learn from each other's scriptures and faiths when we learn to accept each other as we are and to appreciate the traditions that God gave us.

Notes

1. For the lexical meanings and derivations of the term *millah*, see Edward W. Lane, *An English-Arabic Lexicon* (Beirut: Librarie du Liban, 1980), s.v. *millah*.

2. *Ta'rīkh al-rusul wa-al-mulūk*. See the impressive English translation of this work in multiple volumes published as *The History of al-Tabarī* (Albany: State University of New York Press, 1987-1999), especially vols. 1 and 2, which deal with ancient biblical history.

3. See Q 3:26 and 140; for different interpretations of these verses, see Mahmoud M. Ayoub, *The Qur'an and Its Interpreters*, vol. 2, *The House of 'Imran* (Albany: State University of New York Press, 1992), 73ff. and 326ff.

4. Cf. Ps. 37:29, "The righteous shall inherit the land and live in it forever" (New Revised Standard Version).

5. See the Prolegomena to his history of the Arabs and Berbers, Ibn Khaldun, *The Muqaddimah: An Introduction to History*, 3 vols., trans. Franz Rosenthal (Princeton, N.J.: Princeton University Press, 1967), vol. 1.

6. Patricia Crone and Michael Cook, *Hagarism: The Making of the Islamic World* (Cambridge, UK/New York: Cambridge University Press, 1977).

7. For different interpretations of this verse, see Mahmoud M. Ayoub, *The Qur'an and Its Interpreters*, 1:264-66.

8. See Ayoub, *The Qur'an and Its Interpreters*, 2:238-40.

9. Muslim traditionists have interpreted the term *Ahmad* to refer to the holy spirit. See 'Abd al-Malik Ibn Hisham, *The Life of Muhammad*, trans. Alfred Guillaume (Lahore, India: Oxford University Press, 1970).

10. Most translations, however, refer to the descendants of Abraham as "families" rather than nation.—Eds.

11. The Qur'an neither mentions Nimrod by name nor identifies

him as king, but later tradition wrongly identifies him with the Nimrod of Genesis, who is described as a "mighty hunter before the Lord" (see Gen. 10:9). For a discussion of Nimrod in the Islamic tradition, see *The History of al-Tabarī*, vol. 2, *Prophets and Patriarchs*, trans. William M. Brinner (Albany: State University of New York Press, 1987).

12. For a dramatic account of this miracle, see *The History of al-Tabarī*, vol. 2, *Prophets and Patriarchs*, 59ff.

13. Ahmad b. Hanbal, *Musnad Ibn Hanbal*, "Kitab al-shamiyyin," Hadith #16525.

14. *Sahih Muslim*, Kitab I, "Kitab al-iman," Hadith #1.

15. The original German publication was Abraham Geiger, *Was hat Mohammed aus dem Judenthume aufgenommen?* (1902; Osnabrück: Biblio Verlag, 1971); the English edition appeared as *Judaism and Islam* (New York: Ktav, 1970).

ABRAHAM AND HIS CHILDREN: RESPONSE

MICHAEL L. FITZGERALD

PROFESSOR AYOUB starts his paper with a Qur'anic reference to the fathernood of Abraham. He goes on to say that we, as Jews, Christians, and Muslims, share a father in Abraham in both the physical and the spiritual sense. I would wonder if we do agree on a physical descent from Abraham. While the Jewish people can be said to descend from Abraham, surely there are also groups of judaized people, that is, those who were not originally Jews but adopted the Jewish religion. Cannot the same be said about Muslims? It may be held that the Arabs are descended from Abraham through Ishmael (though, as I mentioned in my paper, this can be called into question), but in any case the vast majority of Muslims are not Arabs. As Professor Ayoub himself says, it is *by extension* that Abraham is the father of Muslims. Certainly for Christians, as Paul, himself a Jew, emphasizes, it is the spiritual descent that counts.

Professor Ayoub rightly underlines the importance of the covenant made with Abraham, while acknowledging that here again the understanding of the covenant differs. For Islam this covenant is a repetition of the one made with the whole of humanity. Its essential content is the recognition by humanity of God's lordship. For Jews the covenant with Abraham concerns primarily the gift of the land. For Christians the covenant concerns Abraham's descent, understood in the singular, as pointing to Christ. Christianity recognizes a succession of covenants: first with Noah, then with Abraham, again with Moses, and finally the New Covenant sealed by the blood of Jesus Christ. The former covenants are not abolished, but are subsumed in the final and definitive covenant.

It is interesting that Ayoub lays stress on the Abrahamic resonances of the *hajj*. It is surely in this living out through liturgical gestures that the faith of Abraham is consolidated in the believer. In my own paper I underlined the role of liturgy as an indication of faith. The Eucharist is linked with the sacrifice of Abraham, yet we could say it goes beyond it. While God spared Abraham's son and substituted a ram for the human sacrifice, according to Christian belief God did not spare his own son, allowing Jesus to die on the cross, but raised him to life again through the resurrection. Here, of course, we have another fundamental difference of belief.

The dynamic character of Abraham is indicated as a feature of the Islamic tradition, particularly in combating idolatry. The Christian tradition does not see Abraham as the champion of monotheism in this way. Nevertheless, the refutation of idolatry, already present in the Hebrew Scriptures, is to be found in the New Testament texts. Paul, for instance, does not mince words when he talks about the pagans. They cannot be excused, since they knew God but refused to honor God. "The more they called themselves philosophers, the more stupid they grew, until they exchanged the glory of the immortal God for a worthless imitation, for the image of mortal man, of birds, of quadrupeds and reptiles" (Rom. 1:22-23). Paul's message is really that without the good news of God's saving grace, offered in Jesus Christ, human beings cannot be saved.

This leads to a further remark connected with the name given to Abraham, *khalil Allah*, the friend of God. Ayoub says that Abraham became "by his own effort" God's intimate friend. I do not think that Christians would agree with this, unless they happened to be Pelagians or neo-Pelagians. The concept of friendship is extremely important, but it is a grace, not something earned. The friendship is established by responding to God in faith. Paul puts this very clearly. Quoting Genesis 15:6, he say: "Abraham put his faith in God, and this faith was considered as justifying him" (Rom. 4:3). It is not so much what Abraham does as what he is that counts. It is not the fulfillment of the Law that earns friendship with God and makes Abraham worthy of the promise. Paul continues: "That is why what fulfills the promise depends on faith, so that it may be a free gift and be available to all of Abraham's descendants, not only those who belong to the Law but also those who belong to the faith of Abraham who is the father of all of us" (Rom. 4:16). Is this not a way of understanding that can unite all of us, Jews, Christians, and Muslims, despite our different understanding of Abraham?

This would seem to be Ayoub's understanding when he goes on to advocate the "dialogue of life." He sees this as a common search for justice, fairness, and peace in the world. He is right to emphasize that this is a lived dialogue rather than pure theory. He mentions fairness. There is truly a continuous need to combat prejudice, to overcome anti-Semitism, anti-Christian attitudes, or Islamophobia. Indeed there is need for common effort to overcome all prejudice against religion as such and to see that religion can play its rightful role in society.

The dialogue of life can lead to a "dialogue of action," which can be understood as a more organized form of action. It may be through the cooperation of Jewish, Christian, and Islamic bodies in giving assistance to the poor, in helping refugees, or in fighting against HIV/AIDS. It may be through common participation in movements such as the World Conference of Religions for Peace. Such cooperation can be at the local level, or it can be national or international. There is room for much initiative.

The dialogue of life and the dialogue of action are to be supported and stimulated by the other two types of dialogue mentioned by Professor Ayoub. There is first the "dialogue of theology and philosophy," what Catholic documents would call "the dialogue of theological exchange." It should be clear that what is intended here is not an argument about who holds the truth, but rather a clarification of ideas leading to greater mutual understanding. This can be a contribution to overcoming prejudice and encouraging cooperation. The second form, "the dialogue of faith," would correspond to the "dialogue of religious experience." This can take the form of a theoretical study of the riches of the respective spiritual heritages, but it can also mean a type of spiritual emulation, as each learns from the other how to respond to God. The greater respect that this promotes can also lead to a more fruitful dialogue of life.

It will not be possible to eliminate the differences. Ayoub points to Christ and Muhammad as the "great obstacles" to Christian–Muslim dialogue. The figure of Abraham, too, is seen to be problematic. Yet are these differences really an obstacle to dialogue? Is it not possible for Christians to try to better understand Muhammad as Muslims see him, and for Muslims to try to understand Christ as Christians see him? Can their respective figures not be seen in connection with the whole system of belief and practice, and its inner logic appreciated? As Muslims would say, *al-hukm li-Llah*, judgment belongs to God alone. It is God, as the Qur'an says, who will judge the differences on the day of resurrection (cf. Q 3:55). Paul, concluding his meditation on the resurrection, puts it in another way: "And when everything is subjected to him, then the Son himself will be subject in his turn to the One who subjected all things to him, so that God may be all in all" (1 Cor 15:28). Cannot all the children of Abraham be united in this Godward march?

Abraham and His Children: RESPONSE

Reuven Firestone

PROFESSOR AYOUB'S PRESENTATION on Abraham is a lesson on ecumenism. He manages to raise and discuss difficult issues in a way that is both challenging and humble. Although Professor Ayoub was never my teacher in the classroom, for many years I have considered him a mentor.

Dr. Ayoub provides a model for Abraham as prototype, and he notes how each religious community tends to feel its deepest connection with only a part of the full person that is Abraham. My own experience confirms his observation every semester that I teach an undergraduate course at the University of Southern California, called "Reading Scripture as Skeptic and Believer," in which we read parallel material found in the Hebrew Bible, New Testament, and Qur'an. We study the Abraham stories because of their importance in each scripture, and when we do so we inevitably observe a fascinating breakdown among students of faith. The Christians tend to see Abraham as the prototype of the person of faith in God (Rom. 4), the Muslims tend to see him as a prototype of the person of submission to the will of God (2:124; 4:125), and the Jews tend to resonate most with Abraham as the prototype of the person who argues, even *with* God (Gen. 18)!

What we are observing in each case, of course, is a purely mono-scriptural-centric view of the patriarch/prophet. I find that students of faith tend to resist expanding the image and meaning of Abraham when that image is found in the scripture of another faith. Sometimes they find themselves in an awkward position when, after arguing against a perspective of Abraham found in the verses of another scripture, they are shown where the same image may be found elsewhere in the scripture they consider their own! The problem, as articulated by Professor Ayoub, is the difficulty we have accepting the authenticity of each other's scripture and faith.

The late Professor Marilyn Waldman taught that we must all be willing to accept at least the *possibility* of divine truth in the revelation of the other. And I would add to this that *not* doing so is simply an expression of arrogance. How can I have the audacity to declare that billions of Christians and Muslims throughout history have been foolishly duped into believing a lie that is their scripture?

Part of the problem with the study of scripture across religious and scriptural boundaries is our tendency toward a binary approach. We are taught to use such words as "truth" when we read scripture. But this word is dichotomous. When we use such language as truth, we must naturally presume that whatever is not "truth" is "lies."

I believe deeply in the divine or divinely inspired teaching of my own faith's revelation. Its depth, its miraculous ability to reach deeply into our souls and force many of us to examine our own lives and behaviors, its pathos, wisdom, humor, concern, even anger, mercy, and compassion—all reflect, for me, a unity of wisdom within one great God. But the medium of all scriptural revelation—the mode by which we come to know it—is the human medium of writing (and its ancillary products such as computers, etc.).[1] This is human and divine interaction. The product of "scribing" revelation into scripture is a combination of human effort with the divine word, and any endeavor that includes human input is destined to have rough edges and even mistakes.

I cannot accept the dogma of immutability of any scripture. The discovery at Nag Hammadi and elsewhere of additional narrations of the gospel attributed to Thomas, Mary Magdalene, and others demonstrates clearly to me the human side of the New Testament. The unavoidable acceptance of certain variants in the Torah, the most sacred part of scripture for Jews, demonstrates the Jewish acknowledgment that the Hebrew Bible has been affected by scribal error. It would improve interreligious dialogue if Muslims were able to acknowledge at least the possibility that the Qur'an is also a joint product of God and humanity. We have the evidence from early Islamic texts and tradition, but critical study of scripture has not yet become very acceptable in the Islamic world.

My course at USC has taught me that we tend to apply different criteria to our reading of the scripture of other religious traditions than we do to our own. We tend to assume, a priori and dogmatically, that our scripture represents truth while theirs does so only insofar as it conforms to our own. I have had religious students who succeeded brilliantly in their critical reading of other scripture but were unable to apply the same critical eye to their own. I understand the difficulty such students face, for I am confronted with similar issues nearly every day. But to me, applying different analytical criteria to different scriptures is both disingenuous and harmful, for it leads people astray from the divine wish for human understanding and peace.

My religious tradition wisely teaches that no one has the wisdom to really know the divine will. We are taught from a young age to struggle with the text, to keep learning, to argue over the meanings of words and ideas of scripture. But the religious quest in Judaism is confined to our own scripture and religious writings, and this, in my opinion, is an error. As Dr. Ayoub has taught us, Abraham is a model for God's creation of the religious person, but we are capable of seeing only a part of the total Abraham. For us to learn truly what God expects of the person of faith, we need to engage in dialogue, not only through discussion with persons of different faiths but also through dialogue with their sacred texts. By reading and discussing with Christians and Muslims what God teaches about Abraham in their scriptures, I am able to form a more complete picture of the meaning of his life and, therefore, the meaning of my own. With help from my Christian and Muslim religious compatriots I am helped to understand more fully not only the religious experience of another person of religion but also my own personal faith.

Note

1. I am aware of Qur'an 96, which teaches how God teaches with a pen, but though the gift of writing may have been given or inspired by God, it has become a thoroughly human mode of expression. The three great revelations of Judaism, Christianity, and Islam were all conveyed orally (with the possible exception of the Ten Utterances of Exod. 20/Deut.) and reduced to writing only at a date after revelation.

ABRAHAM AND HIS CHILDREN: REPLY

MAHMOUD M. AYOUB

I HAVE HAD THE PLEASURE of Professor Firestone's friendship since his student days. I have always been impressed with his intellectual curiosity and courage and his honesty and humility. The test of our dialogical relationship happened when a few years ago we participated in a public conversation on the significance of Abraham for Muslims and Jews. I suggested that we switch roles, so that Reuven would introduce the Abraham of the Islamic tradition and I would speak about the Abraham of the Hebrew Bible and the midrashic tradition. The result was a memorable experience of ecumenical and scholarly dialogue, marked with respect, understanding, and appreciation of each other's traditions.

Let me get into the substance of his response. I have a problem with Firestone's interpretation of the significance of Abraham for Jews. Abraham did not "argue with God," but pleaded with God to spare the two cities. To argue with someone is to contend with him or her as an equal rival. So how could Abraham have contended with God when he says, "I will speak with the Lord, but I am nothing but dust and ashes" (Gen. 18:27)? Firestone's view, I believe, reflects some aspects of modern Jewish humanism and midrashic tradition rather than the biblical Abraham, who is a model of humble obedience to the divine will and recipient of God's covenant.

Professor Firestone raises the most crucial question for all those who are interested in interfaith dialogue when he asks, "How can I have the audacity to declare that billions of Christians and Muslims throughout history have been foolishly duped into believing a lie, that is their scriptures?" The answers to this question have been the greatest obstacle in the way of understanding and peace among Abraham's children.

Three broad attitudes of Jews, Christians, and Muslims seem to dominate their dialogical efforts in recent decades. The first is an attitude of indifference: let everyone believe what they want, as long as they leave us alone. Traditionally, this has been the Jewish attitude toward the followers of all other religions, but especially toward Christians and Muslims. The second is an attitude of condescending tolerance of Muslims in particular, which is generally the liberal Christian attitude. The third is one of aggressive missionary activity, based on the conviction that the other is indeed duped into believing a lie and, therefore, must be converted to our position, which is the only and absolute truth. Expressed in different ways, this has traditionally been the attitude of conservative Muslims and Christians toward anyone who is not of their own persuasion.

Dr. Firestone proposes a fourth position, one with which I am in general agreement. There certainly is a need to dialogue not only with followers of other faiths, but also with their scriptures. This, however, implies respect not only for the scriptures themselves, but for their sanctity and significance in the lives of their devotees. Muslims have from the beginning studied the Qur'an critically with regard to its language and meaning. Therefore, to ask them to doubt the divine origin of the Qur'an is to ask them to abandon Islam as a faith and a worldview, or at least to question the foundation of their faith. It is like asking Christians to be Christians without Christ.

Professor Firestone is, I am sure, aware of the fact that Muslims have always accepted the human role in the "scribing" of their scripture. They have even accepted variants in the wording of the revelation, as indicated in the science of readings (*qira'at*) and the traditions of the "seven modes" of revelation. Unless the Qur'an is from God, it will have no authority or power over the lives of billions of Muslims who were shaped and dominated by it. What is at issue for me, and for many other Muslims, is the relationship of the Qur'an to human history and to the life and mission of Muhammad, the prophet of Islam. But such issues do not question the basic conviction that the Qur'an was revealed by God.

Finally, Reuven's challenging statement, "Applying different criteria to different scriptures is both disingenuous and harmful," calls for comment. This is true when Muslims insist on judging both the Hebrew Bible and New Testament by the criteria of Qur'anic revelation, and when Jews and Christians fall into the same pit. I believe that we must all respect the scriptures of the other, as well as the place that scripture holds in the lives of the other. In this way, it is hoped, we can better discern the "divine wish for human understanding and peace."

Archbishop Fitzgerald raises many important issues in his response to my essay. I want first to express my appreciation for the spirit of his response. He tends, however, to take some of my remarks more literally than they are meant to be taken.

I have dealt with his doubt about the Ishmaelitic descent of the Arabs in my response to his essay. Suffice it to say here that Abraham is more than the metaphorical father of Jews, Christians, and Muslims. When some Jews denied Jewish converts the right to this paternity, the great Rabbi Musa bin Maymun defended this right in his famous epistle to the Jews of the Yemen. It seems that St. Paul's remarks about Abraham who is "the father of all of us" also go far beyond a metaphysical idea. Abraham is a living patriarch for all of us; he is our father of faith.

Ibrahim, the Arabic name for Abraham, has been interpreted by later tradition to mean "*ab Rahim*," a compassionate father. Abraham and his wife Sarah will act in paradise as parents to orphans who die young. In this way Abraham is a father to those who have no father. He is the embodiment of the Qur'anic injunction to care for the orphans and the needy. But above all, Abraham is our father in true *islam* to God. I believe that Christians come close to this Islamic idea in the gospel notion of the "bosom of Abraham" (Luke 16:19-31, esp. v. 23), where the poor of this world, like Lazarus, will have a compassionate father.

Archbishop Fitzgerald takes issue with my linking Abraham's covenant with the Qur'anic primordial divine covenant with humanity. He wishes to limit the Abrahamic covenant to the gift of the holy land. This of course ignores the covenant of blessing, "Through your seed all the nations of the earth shall be blessed" (Gen. 12:3b). To limit the seed of Abraham to Christ is to deny both the Jews and Muslims their Abrahamic heritage. Likewise, to assert that the covenants with Abraham and other prophets of the Hebrew Bible "were subsumed in the final and definitive covenant . . . sealed by the blood of Jesus Christ" is to subordinate Abraham's role to the Christian soteriological mission of Jesus. Again, this renders meaningless the biblical, midrashic, and Qur'anic personality of Abraham as the obedient friend of God and faithful idol breaker.

Archbishop Fitzgerald rightly notes the importance of the liturgy as a means of sharing in the rich heritage of Abraham. There is, I believe, nothing in the Jewish liturgical binding (*Akedah*) of Isaac that would negate either the Christian or Islamic claims to Abraham. Similarly, Abraham could have built the Ka'bah and instituted the *hajj* pilgrimage and still play his theological, liturgical, and hagiographical role in Judaism and Christianity. No one denies to Christians the right to see a theological and liturgical link between the sacrifice of Abraham's son and the Eucharist, and hence with the cross of Christ. But to insist that this fundamental difference of belief between Christianity and the two other Abrahamic traditions is definitive and absolutely final is to close the door to theological dialogue. Religion has been most creative when it has spoken in poetry, allegory, and myth. Perhaps we need a new theology that speaks the language of myth and allegory, a language that is open to translation into other religious languages. In this way Abraham, our father, can also become our teacher.

If we deny or undermine the place of Abraham's monotheistic faith in our religious heritage, as Archbishop Fitzgerald seems to suggest, then what does it mean to speak of the "Abrahamic traditions?" In fact, Christians from Jesus and Paul to Augustine and other church fathers and on to Søren Kierkegaard have seen in Abraham's submission to the one God an example of righteous faith. Archbishop Fitzgerald's citation of Paul's critique of the philosophers does not necessarily argue against the significance of Abraham's monotheism.

I am neither an Ash'arite Muslim nor a Lutheran Christian. I believe that, by the grace of God, Abraham earned the status of intimate friendship with God. I did not mean in my remarks to favor free will over predestination, but to reflect on Abraham as the intimate friend (*khalil al-rahman*) of the all-merciful God. Abraham's friendship with God can and should urge all people of faith to strive for this high honor through God's grace and our righteous works.

Archbishop Fitzgerald's remarks on dialogue and especially what I called "the dialogue of life" add depth and richness to my humble ideas, for which I thank him. More than ever before we now need concerted interfaith and international action against fanaticism, bigotry, and hatred. Above all, we need to work for a just world, because injustice on all levels of our lives is the greatest evil. In the quest for justice, the dialogues of life, of theology, and of faith meet.

Finally, I agree with Archbishop Fitzgerald that for dialogue to prosper and guide us in our quest to understand and do the will of God, we must leave the issues of the truth of the prophethood of Muhammad for Christians and divinity of Christ for Muslims for God to judge on the day of resurrection. On this both the Qur'an and New Testament agree. Nevertheless, these issues must not be beyond the limits of dialogue. The divine spirit that God breathed into our first parents is still in us. That Christ possessed this spirit in special abundance is not foreign to the Qur'an. Christ is called in the Qur'an *ruh allah* (Spirit of God). Likewise, prophethood is a gift that God bestowed on many of his servants. That God bestowed it on Muhammad in a measure that allowed him to change the face of world history is a historical fact that should not threaten the truth of any other religious tradition. May the faith of Abraham, the spirit of Christ, and the prophetic genius of Muhammad continue to guide us to the good and to God.

5

Submitting to the Will of God

*Jews, Christians, and Muslims
Learning from Each Other*

IRFAN A. OMAR

AT THE DAWN of the twenty-first century, Jews, Christians, and Muslims are drawn together to confront one of the most difficult challenges yet faced. Each religion has seen a sharp rise in the expression of extremist ideologies that attempt to define the respective traditions within narrow confines, usually characterized by cultural exclusivism, moral shallowness, and theological fundamentalism. Such views are indeed a challenge as we live in increasingly multicultural communities around the world, but they pose an even greater threat to the adherents of each faith who do not wish to share such a narrow vision.

This sense of crisis has generated a call to participate in a concerted effort by many to build alliances that cut across religious traditions, cultures, nations, and ethnic differences and thus defy exclusivist and bigoted claims made in the name of any religious tradition. Characterizations such as "the age of terrorism" and hopeful slogans like "the age of dialogue" have marked our entry into the twenty-first century. However, by the very nature of events and their interpretations in the media, the former is being used far more often than the latter.

The present volume represents an attempt to emphasize the fact that many believers, in this case, in the Abrahamic traditions, are united to combat the narrow visions found within their own heritages. These traditions, through such voices as those of Reuven Firestone, Michael Fitzgerald, and Mahmoud Ayoub, are committed to finding common paths to peace and justice through dialogue.

A Shared History of Growth

A paradigm in which Jews, Christians, and Muslims may be viewed historically is one in which these traditions learn from and grow in relation to each other. It is not necessary for me to invoke the well-known Buddhist truth claim that "all things are connected," because in this case it is apparent that Judaism, Christianity, and Islam have been inextricably linked with one other through much of their respective histories. One may go so far as to say that Judaism, Christianity, and Islam are what they are because of their historical interactions. Judaism and Christianity grew from the narratives of a shared history. They developed closely in relation to and perhaps by way of reacting to each other in the first decades of Christianity's inception. Growing out of the "same mold," they were shaped into their distinct identities as Pauline Christianity and Rabbinic Judaism. Both continue to revere the Hebrew Bible as the word of God.[1]

Throughout the medieval period, Christianity and Islam reacted to each other, shaping and giving direction to the other in completely unexpected and unintended ways, leading to a shared heritage of both conflict and convergence. Muslims and Christians experienced both positive and negative responses through their interaction with the other. Christians who lived under Muslim political rule, although tolerated under Islamic law, often felt politically subjugated. At the same time, Christians also served as models of holiness for many Muslims. Even as Western Christianity experienced Islam through the eyes of the Crusades, the positive impact of Arabic sciences and philosophy resulted in unexpected historical moments of Christian–Muslim unity. In medieval Spain, Christian, Jewish, and Muslim scholars and philosophers worked closely together to nurture a civilization centered on learning and the arts. In the realm of popular religious piety, Christian and Muslim communities from Lebanon to Indonesia continue to share saints, pilgrimage sites, and even a common language and culture.

Similarly, Islam was often seen as Judaism's "spiritual cousin," and adherents of the two lived in relative peace throughout the medieval as well as the modern periods.[2] There is a certain affinity between Islam and Judaism in matters of their treatment of scriptures and their view of history, as well as in their adherence to religious law. Politically, Jews overall felt safer under Islam than under Christian rule. Although the situation was often far from perfect, they thrived within Muslim culture. Moses Maimonides, the famous Jewish philosopher, felt at home in an Arabic-speaking milieu, and in fact read Aristotle through Arabic translations and through the works of the tenth-century Arab philosopher al-Farabi. Thus, there was a significant exchange of ideas and mutual development, particularly in Spain, between the twelfth and thirteenth centuries. Medieval culture and civilization were in fact the result of this sustained interaction among Jews, Christians, and Muslims that ultimately led to the flowering of an age of learning and discovery in various disciplines such as philosophy, mathematics, medicine, and comparative religion.[3] Chronologically last of the three, the Islamic tradition owes a great deal to Judaism and Christianity. In fact, Islam acknowledges these traditions in its scriptures and accords them a theological as well as communal status equal to its own, recognizing both the legitimacy of their claims to divine revelation and their status as religious communities with their own religious laws and regulations.[4] Between the seventh and the ninth centuries there were many levels of interaction among Muslims, Christians, and Jews, mainly in the Arab lands where these communities had lived prior to Muslim rule. Muslims learned from these encounters, often collaborating with their Jewish and Christian counterparts in many respects, most notably in the cultivation of scholastic traditions, which in turn continued to influence and benefit members of all three faiths for centuries.[5]

Although the paradigm I spoke of above involved many positive levels of interaction that resulted in mutual growth at various moments in the shared history of these three world religions, it would be impossible not to think of the numerous conflicts that mark this history as well—conflicts of which we all are well aware. While this part of the history cannot be ignored, I do see this same paradigm of mutual learning and growth reflected in these essays by Firestone, Fitzgerald, and Ayoub. However, there is one major distinguishing feature of their work. Unlike the medieval interactions, the current exchange—building on decades of work by numerous scholars and activists from various traditions—is part of a determined effort to engage the other in a dialogue of equals.

We have come a long way from the medieval paradigm. The current interaction and engagement represent a dialogical approach that is far more structured and intentional about its objectives than any previous encounter. This approach not only takes into account the provision of mutual learning and growth, it also entertains the idea of moving further toward greater recognition of other faiths. It is this dialogical approach that informs the three main essays from a Jewish, a Christian, and a Muslim scholar. Each author presents historical and theological rationales for his particular view of the "other" by way of acknowledging past interactions between them. Furthermore, the contributions of the essays rest on the hope that the effort will lead to a continuing mutual exchange, sharing, and learning among the believers of these three faiths and others who share similar concerns. To this end, the present volume has gone further than merely including the perspectives of the other as they are found in the three Abrahamic traditions. The authors not only present their initial ideas on the main theme, namely, the relationship of the three Abrahamic traditions in light of their understandings of Abraham, but they also engage with each other by responding to the other two. Finally, each author also writes a reply to the responses. As mentioned in the preface, this constitutes a "written form of trialogue"—a complete circle of conversation that took place over the course of several months and across great distances.

It has been argued that some of the earliest initiatives for dialogue came from the humanist, non-Christian philosophies of the eighteenth and nineteenth centuries rather than from any religious impulse. For example, the German scholar Klaus Hock states that the urge to dialogue with non-European religions first found its basis in extratheological principles that were appropriated by Christians as an alternate way to carry on "outreach" to Muslims. The primary reason for this enterprise was that while Islam as a religion could not be recognized as a valid religious path—in the nineteenth-century European perspective there could be only one such path and that was Christianity—there were vast numbers of Muslims in the world who had to be located in the Eurocentric worldview. The rationale for relations with Muslims was thus formulated within a religious missionary perspective; in the postcolonial period, though, it was expanded to include secular perspectives. Thus, the twentieth-century Christian theological understanding of Islam, fragmented as it was, was based not on theological or religious ideals but on modern Western secular values.[6]

Christians began to see Muslims as non-Christian peoples rather than as fellow monotheist believers worshiping the same God. While theological encounters between Christians and Muslims are relatively recent, Christian interest in and understanding of Judaism, particularly the theological engagement between the two traditions in the spirit of dialogue and harmony, began much earlier.[7] Thus, there is a fundamental difference between some of the earliest initiatives for Christian–Muslim dialogue and the beginnings of Jewish–Christian dialogue. The former began as a humanistic endeavor emanating mainly out of Christian humanism of nineteenth-century Europe, while the latter was a theological enterprise from the start since the sharing of scripture was seen as one of the major reasons for mutual understanding.

Similarly, Jewish–Muslim dialogue got off to a late start and advanced very slowly, at least in comparison to the formal as well as informal Jewish–Christian dialogues conducted throughout the 1960s and 1970s and continuing into the present. In this regard, as noted in the opening essay by Bradford Hinze, the efforts made over the past few decades in developing a theological dialogue (bilateral as well as trilateral) are invaluable and are indeed encouraging for any future course of action. To some degree, they compensate for the lack of attention given to theological considerations in those earlier interactions, at least as far as the Muslim–Christian and Muslim–Jewish parts of the trialogue are concerned.

It is important to note that the dialogical approach envisions a conversation among not just those Jews, Christians, and Muslims who happen to be neighbors in the immediate sense of the word but also among those who are "neighbors" in a global sense. As the globe is shrinking, it is bringing these neighbors into contact with each other through travel and rapid means of communication. As contacts among Jews, Christians, and Muslims of the world continue to be politicized and conflict-laden, there is a need to revive and vigorously promote the *many* conversations among people of these three great faiths. These interactions and dialogues need not be limited to scholars but should also include activists, doctors, engineers, lawyers, and even missionaries. A dialogical approach to mutual learning must be promoted at all levels of society and across all disciplines.

Self-disclosure as a Means to Self-knowledge

Even though the process of dialogue has matured over the last few decades and the world has become a better place as a result of a relative openness to each other, dialogue is still ambiguous to many. It is used and appropriated in various ways. To some, dialogue is part and parcel of the missionary effort—yet another tool to attract the attention of those who believe in something different. Some see dialogue as an effective medium for public relations for a particular religious tradition. Others engage in dialogue because they feel pressured, perhaps even threatened, by how they would be portrayed if they failed to show their willingness to dialogue. All these approaches are somewhat self-serving, motivated as they are by something other than the first major objective for dialogue—*learning about the other and, through the other, learning about oneself.* Dialogue, when conducted with complete openness and humility, the twin traits of true dialogue, brings knowledge of the self that cannot be brought about by any other means. It opens up ways of seeing that would not be otherwise known.

When one attempts self-disclosure in dialogue, it is usually undertaken in the spirit of mutual growth and learning. It is also done when one feels a sense of trust in those others who will witness such disclosure. Trust allows all parties involved to share about themselves in a way that is authentic and meaningful. By extending the right of self-definition to all, each party gains knowledge about the other, and each participant also gains a certain perspective about oneself through the other. This is because we often see ourselves in a different light when we consciously project ourselves to others. The beauty of dialogue is that as others gain a greater understanding of our own perspective, we also have an opportunity to grow in how we perceive our self. True self-learning takes place when we are among those who are *not* like us. As is evident from the chapters above, all three authors, Firestone, Fitzgerald, and Ayoub, seemed to engage each other in the conviction that dialogue helps increase mutual knowledge.

An essential component of self-realization through dialogue is a willingness to be honest about one's tradition, its history, and its theology. One should avoid apologetics and self-promotion. It is important to acknowledge mistakes, as Pope John Paul II did on more than one occasion, stating that "Catholics have not always been peacemakers."[8] Similarly, Muslims and Jews as well must acknowledge their own less-than-glorious moments in history. Learning from each other becomes possible when one is able to acknowledge one's own prejudices and biases. Each partner in dialogue must critically examine his or her own tradition's role in misrepresenting as well as in dehumanizing the other both now and in the past.⁹ We can learn from each other only when we are willing to learn from our own mistakes.

History has witnessed some of the most horrible crimes against humanity committed either in the name of religion or by way of appropriation of it. As Firestone aptly notes, each religious community's history has had its low moments, the moments of "worst calamity" that seemed to disintegrate its very core and threaten to dilute the moral fabric of the tradition.¹⁰ Each religious community, then, is responsible for introspection in order to avoid such calamities in the future and to ensure the religious dignity of the self as well as of others. For Muslims, Firestone continues, the worst calamity was not in the thirteenth or the fifteenth or even the nineteenth century—it is being lived out in the present, in what unfortunately has been termed as the "age of terrorism." There is some agreement between what Firestone said and what a number of Muslim leaders and scholars have been saying in recent decades in their calls for greater introspection within Muslim societies, especially with respect to the issue of violence.¹¹ In the end, each community will have to engage in its own self-examination.

Humanizing Dialogue: Recognizing the Other

It is a given that dialogue means different things to different people. For some, dialogue is a means to an end; for others it is an end in itself. Eugene Blake defines dialogue as not merely talking with one another but rather as "a living relationship in which we as individuals and communities lose our suspicion, fear and mistrust of each other, and enter into new confidence, trust and friendliness."¹² Others have added that "true dialogue presupposes that the participants have no intention of changing the other's religion nor even of instilling doubts regarding the faith of the others."¹³ Dialogue is a form of "sharing" that involves not only listening but arriving at a certain understanding. In other words, it is a free and open exchange of meaningful communication between two or more individuals. A similar perspective has been expressed by the Catholic theologian Hans Küng, for whom the goal of any interreligious encounter is to establish communication through a "genuine dialogue conducted with accurate knowledge and trust with a view to long-range effects." Such a dialogue is often marked with complete openness, which in Küng's mind is a stage that transcends tolerance.[14]

This openness is possible only when we are able to humanize dialogue by entering into it to hear other human beings in conversation; this is opposed to thinking of dialogue as "a confrontation between ideas."[15] Dialogue must be preceded by one's commitment to its second major objective: *the acknowledgment and recognition of the other as they are*. This recognition implies that each participant approaches the other as a feeling, thinking, believing human being. No one person must assume that the ideals of his or her tradition, however noble they may be, somehow surpass the humanity of the other. This recognition does not imply that one must agree with the position others have taken, nor should they be prevented from defining themselves. Instead, a key expectation in dialogue is simply to acknowledge that others may have a different perspective and that they also have the right to share and explain that different perspective. Thus, dialogue requires that each person recognize the right of others to self-definition.

The spirited exposition in the present volume of how Abraham is viewed in Judaism, Christianity, and Islam, as well as the discussion that follows about the nature of the relationship of each tradition to the other two, makes one thing clear. Each must receive recognition from the other for being a legitimate tradition that possesses the right to self-definition. In the spirit of advancing dialogue, *it is imperative that they recognize each other's tradition as one of multiple paths to the same goal*. For the Abrahamic traditions this common goal is submission to the will of one God. Implicit in mutual recognition of the right to self-definition is our willingness to accept what Firestone calls "at least the *possibility* of divine truth in the revelation of the other."[16] This acceptance of the possibility of truth in the other's tradition does not imply repudiating belief in the truth of one's own tradition, nor does it mean adherence to a syncretistic view of religion. It is to give to the other what one expects to receive from the other. Recognition must be given if it is to be received. This acceptance can be conceived as a third major objective of dialogue. Simply put, it is recognition of another's tradition as a version of the truth.

This issue of recognizing the tradition of the other or others can be viewed from various perspectives. As far as recognizing the validity of other scriptures is concerned, a complex relationship exists among them. While Christians revere and see the Hebrew Scriptures as part of their own tradition, the reverse is not true for Jews. Muslims accept the scriptures of the Jews and the Christians while rejecting their current form, arguing that they have been subjected to interpolation and therefore can no longer be regarded as authentic. Neither Christians nor Jews view the Qur'an as divine revelation. Christians in general have recognized the "spirituality" of Muslims, as Fitzgerald (pp. 60, 67-70) informs us with reference to the Second Vatican Council document *Nostra Aetate*. However, *Nostra Aetate* does not regard Islam as a valid spiritual and religious path, nor does it speak of Muhammad, the prophet of Islam, or the Qur'an. In the view of Christians, Muslims remain outside of "God's saving grace," having rejected the divinity of Jesus Christ.[17]

Similarly, Ayoub acknowledges in his essay (p. 108) that Muslims accept the Christianity of the Qur'an, which, among other things, rejects the divinity of Jesus Christ, giving him instead the status of a special prophet. This leads Muslims to also reject Christians. Popular opinion in Muslim scholarship is that Jesus' teachings were distorted and therefore the practices prevalent in the name of Jesus Christ today are not the ones taught by him.[18] Most notably at the heart of this debate is the concept of the Trinity, which Muslims regard as *shirk* (idolatry), a major sin according to Islamic law. The Muslim acceptance of Judaism is similar to its acceptance of Christianity. In addition, during the last few decades, the political conflict in Israel/Palestine has given rise to a range of anti-Jewish literature in the Muslim world that seeks to dehumanize Jews and includes rather extremist and denigrating views of their religion.

As Fitzgerald rightly observes, the Abrahamic religions have "asymmetrical" (p. 64) views of each other, but this need not necessarily translate into taking a polemical stance against the other traditions. Firestone and Ayoub fully agree as well that while striving to go beyond polemics, partners in dialogue must not try to reduce the particularities of the traditions. Indeed, there are differences, and perhaps they will remain there for good. However, this must not deter members of these faiths from continuing to come together in dialogue for the sake of mutual understanding and growth and, above all, for the purpose of collaborating on the many problems that confront all human beings. As responsible believers in God, we must recognize our role on earth as peacemakers in dialogue with one another. Such collaboration of religions is particularly needed to eliminate bigotry, injustice of all kinds, and foremost of all, violence, which is often waged in the name of ideologies, religious or secular.

In the end what matters most is not our belief in one set of ideals or the other, but what we bring to the world in living out those ideals. I believe that sincere efforts to dialogue with others can make us better instruments of peace and justice as we begin to recognize differences for what they are within the larger context of our common humanity. Therefore, our engagement in dialogue must not be simply for the sake of comparing notes on similarities and differences, nor should it be pursued as merely an intellectual exercise between scholars. Dialogue should be aimed at sustaining the ethical and moral character of society and its individuals. In this, all three Abrahamic traditions provide ample resources from both their scriptures and the examples of countless believers in history.

The main objectives of dialogue revolve around our sincere efforts to generate a spirit of mutual understanding, recognition, and cooperation as well as to recover what Fitzgerald calls "a sense of God" (p. 74) by constantly guarding against becoming arrogant. All three perspectives on Abraham presented herein agree that Abraham did indeed submit to the will of God and in this process he acquired humility. This striving to attain a sense of God, which in turn generates humility, must involve a "sense of humanity" as well, because the experience of God the creator begins with our experience with and reverence for the creation. In other words, our efforts to recover a sense of God must translate into our respect for human rights, our care for the environment, our willingness to fight for economic and social justice, and, above all, our united front against all forms of violence in the world. Dialogue at this level gives meaning to the lives of those who are directly engaged in it but also to those who benefit only indirectly from such efforts. Thus, Ayoub rightly calls this a "dialogue of life" (pp. 105-6), in which members of each community, inspired by the teachings of their respective traditions, direct their energies not merely toward verbalizing their respect for life but also to engaging in "common action" (p. 75) on behalf of the oppressed and those in need.

The three essays by Firestone, Fitzgerald, and Ayoub discuss Abraham and his "pure faith" in God as well as what this means in their respective faiths. Despite problems in understanding and huge differences in interpretation, each of the three essays concludes with the optimism quite characteristic not only of Abraham and Sarah but also of Hagar, Ishmael, and Isaac. Each of them endured immense problems and overcame them with the help of God. Similarly, the three authors are hopeful and seek peace among themselves as well as between them and the world. Implicitly, and sometimes quite explicitly, they call for action to make the world more peaceful and just. Each of the three Abrahamic traditions represents Abraham's hope for his progeny. As we all invoke Abraham's true faith as a sign of our spiritual affinity with him, we must also reflect on and be moved by what that faith calls us to do.

Collaborating in the Way of Peace and Justice

Each of the three Abrahamic religions envisages a world in which human beings would actively promote actions oriented toward peace and justice. These actions are expected to be both moral and efficacious, and they rule out the possibility of using unethical means, such as violence, or at least unqualified violence.

There are two kinds of peace—that within an individual, and collective or universal peace. Peace within oneself is fundamental, as the Psalms indicate, "There is no peace in my bones because of my sin" (Ps. 38:3). This implies a certain sense of godliness, which leads to the second kind of peace, collective or universal peace. There are many examples of the teachings of peace and justice in the Jewish tradition, such as the words of the prophet Isaiah: "They shall beat their swords into plowshares and their spears into pruning hooks. Nation shall not lift up sword against nation, neither shall they learn war anymore" (Isa. 2:4). Similarly, Zechariah called on his people to embrace the love for truth and peace: he reminded them in the name of the Lord, "Not by might nor by power, but by my spirit, says the Lord of hosts" (Zech. 4:6). Again, Psalm 34:15 says, "Seek peace, and pursue it." It is not sufficient to wait for peace to happen; the faithful are asked to actively seek it out.

Similarly, the Christian tradition identifies itself with the mission of Jesus Christ, who, Christians believe, was the embodiment of God's will to renew peace and justice on earth. For Christians, Christ established an example of peace as generosity in giving his own life for the sake of others. When his birth was announced by the angels, it was accompanied with such phrases as "Glory to God" and "Peace on earth" (Luke 2:14). In the New Testament this peace is never detached from justice, because "peace includes loving and feeding enemies" (Luke 6:27; Rom. 12:20).

The Islamic scriptures consider actions in the way of peace and justice as a supreme religious duty, thus raising them to the level of prayer and fasting—which are two of the five primary religious obligations for all Muslims. The Qur'an instructs, "O you who believe! Stand out firmly for justice as witnesses to God even though it be against yourselves, or your parents, or your kin, and whether it be against rich or poor for God can best protect both. Follow not the lusts [of your hearts] lest you swerve, and if you distort or decline to do justice, indeed God is well-acquainted with all that you do" (Q 4:135). In order to work for peace and justice, Muslims must make alliances with all those who likewise seek peace and justice in their own various ways. They must search for common ground and share in the means to strive for these important goals. The Qur'an invites, "Say, 'O People of the Book, come to an agreement between us and you, that we shall worship none but God, that we associate no partners with him, that we erect not from ourselves lords and patrons other than God...'" (Q 3:64). Common alliance against injustice and violence requires dialogue with others and certainly with all those who share the common vision of establishing peace and justice. Indeed, God commands in the Qur'an that if one community fails to heed the call to action for the sake of justice, God will raise another,[19] which implies that seeking justice and working to establish peace are the foundation for all religious action. This also entails opening channels of communication and engaging in dialogue with those who are deemed the other.

Conclusion

The ideology of the other usually divides human groups into "them" and "us," where the other seems quite different from "us" in a variety of ways, but, most important of all, in cultural and religious terms. Islam counters any such ideology of the other by highlighting what it calls the unity of all humanity. The Qur'an states that God constituted human beings into communities and nations so as to enable them to recognize one another. The differences that we possess are there so that each human being will see "us" in "them" and "them" in "us," so to speak. In a sense, diversity is humanity's best measure of itself, because it allows one to keep things in perspective. Once the realization occurs that in fundamental terms *they* are no different from *us*, the particularities of each become less significant and the common core of being human guides the rest of the way. This rest of the way has been designated by the Qur'an as an "olympics of good works."[20] Another instance of such Qur'anic emphasis is found in Fazlur Rahman's comments regarding pluralism, where, paraphrasing Q 5:48, he says: "the positive value of different religions and communities ... is that they may compete with each other in goodness."[21] As Ayoub has also argued, the Qur'an, therefore, makes a strong case for dialogue across religious, cultural, national, and social boundaries, as well as for cooperation between all communities working toward a common goal of establishing peace and justice. Similarly, Fitzgerald notes that emulating Abraham implies being open to the needs of others and collectively rediscovering ourselves as members of the same family. Firestone, too, has called for the three monotheistic traditions to end competition and negative posturing against each other and instead to work for peace and the realization of what he calls a "postpolemical age" (p. 37).

Jews, Christians, and Muslims have come a long way in the last few decades in building a foundation for dialogue between their communities. As is evident from the introductory essay, numerous initiatives to gather people from these three traditions around the table have produced invaluable studies for future discussions. These studies have shown that past conversations were by and large honest encounters, free of polemics. Future steps in dialogue should strive to remain within these parameters, without shying away from critical discussion of issues of difference along with issues of similarity and common challenges. While the three traditions have obvious differences, there is a basic unity that Firestone refers to as the "unity of difference" (pp. 37-38), most evident in their faith in the one God, the same God that Abraham and many of his descendants have followed for millennia. The differences are at best marginal and can be maintained without losing common ground within an overarching framework of respect and recognition for all.

Finally, in order to be true heirs of Abraham, and indeed of Sarah and Hagar and Ishmael and Isaac (what Ayoub calls the "total Abraham"), we must be cognizant of the fact that the message they left behind was one of loyalty and complete trust in God. We must be hopeful, therefore—as God indeed wishes us to be—that dialogue will bring understanding and respect for all the peoples of the earth, the Hindus, the Buddhists, and countless others, and not just for the "people of the book," since they too are heirs of Adam, as was Abraham.

Notes

1. *Nostra Aetate* and many subsequent documents clarify as well as affirm the close relationship between Catholic Christianity and Judaism based on a shared scripture, among other things. See *John Paul II and Interreligious Dialogue*, ed. Byron L. Sherwin and Harold Kasimow (Maryknoll, N.Y.: Orbis Books, 1999), and *Jewish-Christian Encounters over the Centuries: Symbiosis, Prejudice, Holocaust, Dialogue*, ed. Marvin Perry and Frederick M. Schweitzer (New York: Peter Lang, 1994).

2. Reuven Firestone, "Jewish Culture in the Formative Period of Islam," in *Cultures of the Jews: A New History*, ed. David Biale (New York: Schocken Books, 2002).

3. Mark Cohen, *Under Crescent and Cross: The Jews in the Middle Ages* (Princeton, N.J.: Princeton University Press, 1994).

4. The Qur'an 3:3 speaks of "confirming" the Law of Moses and the Gospel of Jesus.

5. Tarif Khalidi, *Classical Arab Islam: Culture and Heritage of the Golden Age* (Princeton, N.J.: Darwin Press, 1985); and F. E. Peters, *Allah's Commonwealth: A History of the Near East 600-1100 A.D.* (New York: Simon & Schuster, 1973).

6. Klaus Hock, *Der Islam im Spiegel westlicher Theologie: Aspekte christlich-theologischer Beurteilung des Islams im 20. Jahrhundert* (Cologne/Vienna: Böhlau Verlag, 1986).

7. See, for example, several works of Eugene Fisher on this subject, some of which have been included in the select bibliography of this volume.

8. See *Interreligious Dialogue: The Official Teaching of the Catholic Church (1963-1995)*, ed. Francesco Gioia (Boston: Pauline Books, 1997).

9. Increasingly, what members of each tradition are recognizing as a result of mutual self-growth through dialogue is that all acts of intolerance and injustice carried out in the name of religion must be condemned by the coreligionists of the perpetrators. They should be condemned uncondition-

ally, without apology for the people who have committed them. An important way to preserve the social, moral, and spiritual integrity of a tradition is to engage with it critically and to apply the values it promotes in one's own religious life and to recognize the ways in which these values affect others around us, especially those who are not of the same tradition.

10. Firestone's Reply, 51-52.

11. Besides the numerous religious leaders and scholars throughout the Muslim world, there is a new generation of younger scholars of Islam as well as community leaders in the West who have called for intensive activism to restore such values as respect for human rights, freedom of religion, and political freedom in Muslim societies. See, for example, the writings of Khaled Abou El Fadl, Sohail Hashmi, Ingrid Mattson, Farid Esack, Steven Barboza, A. Rashied Omar, and many others. It must be noted, however, that in many places around the world, Muslims are also subjected to gross violations of these humanistic values for a variety of political and economic reasons, a discussion which is beyond the scope of this essay.

12. Cited in S. J. Samartha and J. B. Taylor, *Christian-Muslim Dialogue: Papers from Broumana, 1972* (Geneva: WCC, 1973), 8.

13. See Maurice Borrmans, *Guidelines for Dialogue between Christians and Muslims*, trans. R. Marston Speight (Mahwah, N.J.: Paulist Press, 1990), 42.

14. Hans Küng, "A Christian Scholar's Dialogue with Muslims," *The Christian Century* 102, no. 30 (October 9, 1985): 892.

15. Mahmoud Ayoub, "Muslim Views of Christianity: Some Modern Examples," *Islamochristiana* 10 (1984): 70.

16. Firestone's Response to Ayoub's essay, 117.

17. Fitzgerald's Response to Ayoub's essay, 112-15.

18. Jane Dammen McAuliffe, *Qur'anic Christians: An Analysis of Classical and Modern Exegesis* (Cambridge: Cambridge University Press, 1991).

19. See, e.g., Q 2:143, 213; 40:9; 47:38.

20. See Ernest Hamilton, "The Olympics of 'Good Works': Exploitation of a Qur'anic Metaphor," *The Muslim World* 81 (January 1991): 72-81. The Qur'anic verse 49:13 continues "the noblest among you in the eyes of God is one who is most righteous."

21. Fazlur Rahman, "A Muslim Response: Christian Particularity and the Faith of Islam," in *Christian Faith in a Religiously Plural World*, ed. Donald G. Dawe and John B. Carman (Maryknoll, N.Y.: Orbis Books, 1980), 74.

Selected Bibliography

Agius, Emmanuel, and Lionel Chircop, eds. *Caring For Future Generations: Jewish, Christian, and Islamic Perspectives.* Westport, Conn.: Praeger, 1998.

Arnaldez, Roger. *Three Messengers for One God.* Translated by Gerald W. Schlabach and Mary Louise Gudé. Preface by David B. Burrell. Notre Dame, Ind.: University of Notre Dame Press, 1994.

Ayoub, Mahmoud. *The Qur'an and Its Interpreters.* Albany: State University of New York Press, 1984, 1992. [Two of four projected volumes have appeared.]

Banki, Judith H., and John T. Pawlikowski, eds. *Ethics in the Shadow of the Holocaust: Christian and Jewish Perspectives.* Franklin, Wis.: Sheed & Ward, 2001.

Bretton-Granatoor, Gary M., and Andrea L. Weiss, eds. *Shalom/Salaam: A Resource for Jewish-Muslim Dialogue.* New York: Urj Press, 1993.

Brown, Stuart E., ed. *Meeting in Faith: Twenty Years of Christian–Muslim Conversations Sponsored by the World Council of Churches.* Geneva: World Council of Churches, 1989.

Burrell, David B. *Freedom and Creation in Three Traditions.* Notre Dame, Ind.: University of Notre Dame Press, 1993.

———. *Knowing the Unknowable God: Ibn-Sina, Maimonides, Aquinas.* Notre Dame, Ind.: University of Notre Dame Press, 1986.

Busse, Heribert. *Islam, Judaism and Christianity: Theological and Historical Affiliations.* Translated by Allison Brown. Princeton, N.J.: Markus Wiener, 1998.

Cohen, Mark. *Under Crescent and Cross: The Jews in the Middle Ages.* Princeton, N.J.: Princeton University Press, 1994.

Croner, Helga, ed. *More Stepping Stones to Jewish-Christian Relations: An Unabridged Collection of Christian Documents 1975-1983.* New York: Paulist Press, 1985.

———, ed. *Stepping Stones to Further Jewish-Christian Relations: An*

Unabridged Collection of Christian Documents. London/New York: Stimulus, 1977.

Doré, Joseph, ed. *Christianisme, judaïsm et islam: Fidélité et ouverture*. Académie internationale des sciences religieuses. Paris: Éditions du Cerf, 1999.

Dulles, Avery, Leon Klenicki, and Edward Idris Cassidy. *The Holocaust, Never to Be Forgotten: Reflections on the Holy See's Document We Remember*. Mahwah, N.J.: Paulist Press, 2001.

Ellis, Kail C., O.S.A, ed. *The Vatican, Islam, and the Middle East*. Syracuse: Syracuse University Press, 1987.

Encounter: Documents for Muslim-Christian Understanding. Rome: Pontifical Institute for Arabic and Islamic Studies. Published monthly since 1974.

al Faruqi, Ismail Raji, ed. *Trialogue of the Abrahamic Faiths*. Herndon, Va.: International Institute of Islamic Thought, 1986.

Firestone, Reuven. *Children of Abraham: An Introduction to Judaism for Muslims*. Jersey City, N.J.: Ktav, 2001.

Fisher, Eugene J. "Christian-Jewish Relations: An Historical Overview and Prognosis." In *Peace, in Deed: Essays in Honor of Harry James Cargas*, edited by Zev Garber and Richard Libowitz, 163-77. Atlanta: Scholars Press, 1998.

———. "Kennedy Institute Jewish–Christian–Muslim Trialogue," *Journal of Ecumenical Studies* 19 (Winter 1982): 197-200.

Fisher, Eugene J., and Leon Klenicki, eds. *In Our Time: The Flowering of Jewish-Catholic Dialogue*. New York: Paulist Press, 1990.

Fisher, Eugene J., and Daniel Polish. *The Formation of Social Policy in the Catholic and Jewish Traditions*. South Bend, Ind.: University of Notre Dame Press, 1980.

———. *Liturgical Foundations of Social Policy in the Catholic and Jewish Traditions*. South Bend, Ind. University of Notre Dame Press, 1983.

Fitzgerald, Michael L., and R. Caspar. *Signs of Dialogue: Christian Encounter with Muslims*. Zamboango City, Philippines: Silsilah Publications, 1992.

Gilbert, Arthur. *The Vatican Council and the Jews*. Cleveland/New York: World Publishing, 1968.

Glick, Leonard B. *Abraham's Heirs*. Syracuse: Syracuse University Press, 1999.

Gordis, David M., George B. Grose, and Benjamin J. Hubbard, eds. *The Abraham Connection: A Jew, Christian, and Muslim in Dialogue*. Notre Dame, Ind.: Cross Cultural Publications, Cross Road Books, 1994.
Gremillion, Joseph B., ed. *Food/Energy and the Major Faiths*. Maryknoll, N.Y.: Orbis Books, 1975.
Gremillion, Joseph B., and William Ryan, eds. *World Faiths and the New World Order: A Muslim–Jewish–Christian Search Begins*. Washington, D.C.: Interreligious Peace Colloquium, 1978.
Groupe de Recherches Islamo-Chrétien. *The Challenge of the Scriptures: The Bible and the Qur'an*. Maryknoll, N.Y.: Orbis Books, 1998.
——. *Foi et Justice: Un défi pour le christianisme et pour l'islam*. Paris: Centurion, 1993.
Haddad, Yvonne Yazbeck, and John L. Esposito, eds. *Daughters of Abraham: Feminist Thought in Judaism, Christianity, and Islam*. Gainesville: University of Florida, 2001.
Haddad, Yvonne Yazbeck, and Wadi Zaidan Haddad, eds. *Christian–Muslim Encounters*. Gainesville: University Press of Florida, 1995.
Heft, James L., ed. *Beyond Violence: Religious Sources of Social Transformation in Judaism, Christianity, and Islam: Abraham Dialogues, 1*. New York: Fordham University Press, 2004.
Institut d'Études Islamo-Chrétiennes. *Déclaration Communes Islamo-Chrétiennes 1954-1995*. Beirut: Dar el-Machreq, 1997.
Institut d'Études Islamo-Chrétiennes. *Déclarations Communes Islamo-Chrétiennes 1995-2001*. Beirut: Dar el-Machreq, 2003.
International Catholic–Jewish Liaison Committee. *Fifteen Years of Catholic–Jewish Dialogue, 1970-1985*. Vatican City: Editrice Vaticana; Rome: Editrice Lateranense, 1988.
Ipgrave, Michael, ed. *The Road Ahead: A Christian-Muslim Dialogue*. London: Church Publishing, 2002.
——, ed. *Scriptures in Dialogue: Christians and Muslims Studying the Bible and the Qur'an Together*. London: Church Publishing, 2004.
Islam & Christian Muslim Relations. Birmingham: Centre for the Study of Islam and Christian–Muslim Relations. Published quarterly since 1990.
Islamochristiana. Rome: Pontifical Institute for Arabic and Islamic Studies. Published annually since 1975; includes bibliography in Arabic, English, and French.
Jewish–Christian Dialogue: Six Years of Christian Jewish Consultations. Geneva: World Council of Churches, 1975.

Keane, Michael. *Believers in One God: Judaism, Christianity, Islam*. Cambridge, Mass.: Cambridge University Press, 1993.
Kuschel, Karl-Josef. *Abraham: A Symbol of Hope for Jews, Christians, and Muslims*. London: SCM Press, 1995.
Kyam, Kristen E., Linda S. Schearing, and Valerie H. Ziegler, eds. *Eve and Adam: Jewish, Christian, and Muslim Readings on Genesis and Gender*. Bloomington: Indiana University Press, 1999.
Levine, Lee I. *Jerusalem: Its Sanctity and Centrality to Judaism, Christianity, and Islam*. New York: Continuum, 1999.
Mojzes, Paul, Leonard Swidler, and Heinz-Gerhardt Justenhoven, eds. *Interreligious Dialogue: Toward Reconciliation in Macedonia and Bosnia*. Philadelphia: Ecumenical Press, 2003; also published in the *Journal of Ecumenical Studies* 39 (2002).
The Muslim World: A Journal Devoted to the Study of Islam and Christian-Muslim Relations. Oxford, UK/Malden, Mass.: Blackwell. Quarterly founded in 1911, published by Hartford Theological Seminary since 1938.
Neusner, Jacob. *Religion and the Political Order: Politics in Classical and Contemporary Christianity, Islam, and Judaism*. Atlanta: Scholars Press, 1996.
Neusner, Jacob, Bruce Chilton, and William Graham. *Three Faiths, One God: The Formative Faith and Practice of Judaism, Christianity, and Islam*. Boston: Brill Academic Publishers, 2002.
Peters, F. E. *Children of Abraham: Judaism, Christianity, Islam*. Princeton, N.J.: Princeton University Press, 1982.
———. *The Monotheists: Jews, Christians, and Muslims in Conflict and Competition*. 2 volumes. Princeton, N.J./Oxford: Princeton University Press, 2003.
Pontifical Biblical Commission. *The Jewish People and Their Sacred Scriptures in the Christian Bible*. Vatican City: Editrice Vaticana; Boston: Pauline Books & Media, 2002.
Pontifical Council for Interreligious Dialogue. *Guidelines for Dialogue between Christians and Muslims*. Mahwah, N.J.: Paulist Press, 1991.
———. *Interreligious Dialogue: The Official Teaching of the Catholic Church (1963-1995)*, edited by Francesco Gioia. Boston: Pauline Books & Media, 1997.
———. *Recognize the Spiritual Bonds Which Unite Us: 16 Years of Christian–Muslim Dialogue*. Vatican City: Pontifical Council for Interreligious Dialogue, 1994.

Proceedings from the Conference of the ICCJ Abrahamic Forum Council. "Convivencia—Enhancing Identity through Encounter between Jews, Christians and Muslims." In *From the Martin Buber House: International Council of Christians and Jews* 29 (2001): 1-233.

Proceedings from the First Conference of the International Council of Christians and Jews (ICCJ) Abrahamic Forum Council. "The Concept of Monotheism in the Abrahamic Traditions." In *From the Martin Buber House: International Council of Christians and Jews* 28 (2000): 1-59.

Race, Alan, and Ingrid Shafer, eds. *Religion in Dialogue: From Theocracy to Democracy*. Hants, UK: Ashgate, 2002.

Samartha, S. J., ed. *Dialogue between Men of Living Faiths: Papers presented at a Consultation at Ajaltoun, Lebanon, March 1970*. Geneva: World Council of Churches, 1971.

———, ed. *Towards World Community: The Colombo Papers*. Geneva: World Council of Churches, 1975.

Scharper, Philip, ed. *Torah and Gospel: Jewish and Catholic Theology in Dialogue*. New York: Sheed & Ward, 1966.

Selengut, Charles, ed. *Jewish–Muslim Encounters: History, Philosophy, and Culture*. New York: Continuum, 2001.

Simpson, William W., and Ruth Weyl. *The Story of the International Council of Christians and Jews* [1946-1995]. Heppenheim, Germany: International Conference of Christians and Jews, Martin Buber House, n.d.

Sperber, Jutta. *Christians and Muslims: The Dialogue Activities of the World Council of Churches and Their Theological Foundation*. Berlin: Walter de Gruyter, 2000.

Swidler, Leonard. *Theoria→Praxis: How Jews, Christians, and Muslims Can Together Move from Theory to Practice*. Leuven: Peeters, 1998.

Vaporis, N. M., ed. *Orthodox Christians and Muslims*. Brookline, Mass.: Holy Cross Orthodox Press, 1986.

Zebiri, Kate. *Muslims and Christians Face to Face*. Oxford, England: Oneworld, 1997.

Internet Resources on Interreligious Dialogue

The **American Islamic Congress** promotes interfaith and interethnic understanding:
http://www.aicongress.org/

The **American Jewish Committee** has a long history of promoting closer interreligious relations in the United States:
http://www.ajc.org/Interreligious/HistoryHighlights.asp

The **American Sufi Muslim Association** (ASMA) Society is devoted to issues of Islamic Culture and Society. The Cordoba Initiative of the ASMA Society advances trialogues among Muslims, Jews, and Christians:
http://www.asmasociety.org/

Caritas Internationalis is a confederation of over 162 Catholic relief and social service agencies that address issues of interfaith conflict and collaboration in peace building:
http://www.caritas.org/

Catholic Relief Services promotes conflict resolution and peace building in situations of interfaith conflict around the world.
http://www. catholicrelief.org/

The **Council of Christians and Jews**:
http://www.ccj.org.uk

Duncan Black Macdonald Center for the Study of Islam and Christian–Muslim Relations:
http://macdonald.hartsem.edu

Fraternité d'Abraham is a French group that meets regularly. Its English-language webpage is:
http://www.fraternitedabraham.com/index_eng.html

The project "**House of Abraham**" sponsored by the World Conference of Religions for Peace began in July 2001:
http://www.haus-abraham.de/

Interfaith Center for Peace:
  http://peace-center.org/
Interfaith Network of the United Kingdom:
  http://www.interfaith.co.uk/
For general information on the **International Council of Christians and Jews**, see:
  http://www.iccj.org/en/
  Also see the **Abrahamic Forum Council** of the International Council of Christians and Jews:
  http://www.iccj.org/en/?id=109
International Interfaith Centre, United Kingdom:
  http://www.interfaith-center.org/oxford/
The **Maimonides Foundation**, a joint Jewish–Muslim interfaith organization:
  http://www.maimonides-foundation.org.uk/
Network of Religious Communities:
  http://www.religiousnet.org/
The **Office of Ecumenical and Interreligious Affairs** of the United States Catholic Conference of Bishops:
  http://www.nccbuscc.org/seia/index.htm
Peace Council:
  http://www.peacecouncil.org/index.html
The **Pontifical Council for Interreligious Dialogue**, Vatican website:
  http://www.vatican.va/roman_curia/pontifical_councils/interelg/index.htm
The **Three Faiths Forum** from the United Kingdom:
  http://www.threefaithsforum.org.uk
The **Trialogue of Cultures** was initiated in 1996 by the Herbert-Quandt-Stiftung in Germany:
  http://www.h-quandt-stiftung.de/
United Religions Initiative:
  http://www.uri.org.uk/
The work of the **World Council of Churches**, with its main offices in Geneva, Switzerland, promotes interreligious relations and dialogue:
  http://www.wcc-coe.org/wcc/what/interreligious/index-e.html

Contributors

MAHMOUD M. AYOUB is originally from South Lebanon. He received his education at the American University in Beirut, the University of Pennsylvania, and Harvard University, where he received his Ph.D. in the history of religions. Since 1988 he has been professor of Islamic Studies at Temple University in Philadelphia. He is also an adjunct professor at the Duncan Black Macdonald Center, Hartford Seminary, Connecticut, and at the Reconstructionist Rabbinical College, Wyncote, Pennsylvania. Professor Ayoub helped develop and launch a graduate program in Christian–Muslim Relations and Comparative Religion at the Centre for Christian–Muslim Studies, University of Balamand, Koura, Lebanon. He also helped formulate and establish the joint Temple-Gajah Mahda Universities comparative religion program in Yogjakarta, Indonesia. Among the many awards and scholarships he has received are the Kent Doctoral Fellowship and the Canada Council Fellowship. He has received Fulbright Fellowships to lecture in Malaysia and for research trips to Egypt and Lebanon. Professor Ayoub has authored many books in the area of Islam and interreligious dialogue. The most notable are *Redemptive Suffering in Islam* and the multivolume work *The Qur'an and Its Interpreters* (2 volumes to date). He has published numerous articles in *The Muslim World*, *Journal of the American Oriental Society*, *Bulletin of the Institute of Middle Eastern Studies*, and *Islamochristiana*. Two of his recent works are *The Crisis of Muslim History: Religion and Politics in Early Islam* (2003) and *Islam in Faith and History* (2004). Currently he is working on the third volume of *The Qur'an and Its Interpreters*.

REUVEN FIRESTONE was born in Santa Rosa, California. He was educated at Antioch College, Hebrew University in Jerusalem, and Hebrew Union College in New York, where he received his M.A. in Hebrew literature in 1980 and his rabbinic ordination in 1982. He received his Ph.D. in Arabic and Islamic Studies from New York University in 1987. From 1987 to 1992 he taught Hebrew literature and directed the Hebrew and Arabic language programs at Boston University. In 1992 he was awarded the Yad Hanadiv

Research Fellowship at Hebrew University, where he spent the year conducting research on holy war in the Islamic tradition. In 2000, Professor Firestone was awarded a fellowship from the National Endowment for the Humanities for his research on holy war in Judaism and was chosen to be a fellow of the Institute for Advanced Jewish Studies at the University of Pennsylvania in 2002. Since 1993 he has served as associate and then full professor of medieval Judaism and Islam at Hebrew Union College in Los Angeles, where he directs the Edgar F. Magnin School for Graduate Studies.

He has authored the following books: *Journeys in Holy Lands: The Evolution of the Abraham-Ishmael Legends in Islamic Exegesis* (1990); *Jihad: The Origin of Holy War in Islam* (1999); *Children of Abraham: An Introduction to Judaism for Muslims* (2001). His articles have appeared in numerous journals including *Journal of Semitic Studies*, *Journal of Near Eastern Studies*, *Journal of Religious Ethics*, *Journal of Jewish Studies*, *Studia Islamica*, *Muslim World*, and others. Professor Firestone is also the founding director of the Institute for the Study of Muslim–Jewish Interrelations (ISMJI) at Hebrew Union College in Los Angeles. ISJMI is collaborating in this effort with University of Southern California and Omar Ibn Al Khattab Foundation of Islamic Studies. The overall aims of ISMJI are to provide scholarships for the study of Jewish–Muslim relations and to foster the study of Judaism and Islam and the study and practice of interfaith relations. This institute also plans to provide numerous opportunities for publication in this field, including the publication of a new *Journal of Jewish-Muslim Relations* and a two-volume series entitled *Understanding Judaism/Understanding Islam*, which will introduce Jews and Muslims to the religion and religious civilization of the other tradition.

ARCHBISHOP MICHAEL L. FITZGERALD was born in Walsall, United Kingdom. An ordained priest in the Society of Missionaries of Africa (White Fathers), he received his doctorate in theology at the Gregorian University in Rome and also has an advanced degree in Arabic from the School of Oriental and African Studies at London University. After teaching in Makerere University, in Kampala, Uganda, and at the Pontifical Institute of Arabic and Islamic Studies in Rome, Archbishop Fitzgerald served in the Sudan for two years. After a period on the General Council of Missionaries of Africa, in 1987 he was named secretary of the Secretariat for Non-Christians, which is now called Pontifical Council for Interreligious Dialogue. In 1991 he was appointed titular bishop of Nepte, and in 2002 he was named president of the Pontifical Council for Interreligious Dialogue and was raised to the rank of archbishop. He has been actively involved in Catholic–Muslim dialogue.

He is the author (with R. Caspar) of *Signs of Dialogue: Christian Encounter with Muslims* (1992) and has numerous articles in journals such as *Concilium, Islamochristiana, Pro Dialogo*, and *Spiritus*. He has also served as a consultant to the Commission for Religious Relations with Jews, and is a member of the Pontifical Council for Promoting Christian Unity. From 1999 to 2002 he served as a member of the Joint Working Group of the Catholic Church with the World Council of Churches.

BRADFORD E. HINZE, an associate professor of theology at Marquette University, received his M.A. in theology from The Catholic University of America and his Ph.D. in theology from the University of Chicago. His areas of specialization are in fundamental and systematic theology in the areas of tradition, ecclesiology, and hermeneutics, in particular as these are influenced by ongoing work on dialogue, and trinitarian theology. He is collaborating with Bernd Jochen Hilberath from the University of Tübingen and Matthias Scharer from the University of Innsbruck on the dialogical and communicative character of theology. Actively involved in the work of the International Network of Societies of Catholic Theology, he is currently its president.

He is the author of *Narrating History, Developing Doctrine: Friedrich Schleiermacher and Johann Sebastian Drey* in the American Academy of Religion Academy Series (1993). He has edited, with D. Lyle Dabney, *Advents of the Spirit: An Introduction to the Current Study of Pneumatology* (2001) and *The Spirit in the Church and the World* (2004). He has published numerous essays in *Theological Studies, Horizons, Heythrop Journal*, and in numerous collected works. He is the author of the forthcoming book *Practices of Dialogue in the Catholic Church: Lessons and Laments*.

IRFAN A. OMAR was educated in India and the United States and is currently an assistant professor of Islam and World Religions at Marquette University. He received his M.A. from Hartford Seminary in Christian–Muslim relations and his Ph.D. in comparative religion from Temple University. His specialization is in Islamic thought with a particular focus on mystical and aesthetic expressions of Islam. His secondary areas of interest are World Religions and South Asian Studies (with a focus on Indian Islam). He has previously taught at Rutgers, Temple, and St. Joseph's Universities. From

1998 to 2002 he was an adjunct professor in the Department of Philosophy and Religion at the College of New Jersey. He served as guest editor for a special issue of *Islam and Christian-Muslim Relations* (Birmingham, England), entitled *Islam in Dialogue* (January 2004), and is currently an associate editor of the *Journal of Ecumenical Studies.*

His recent publications include "Religious Identities and the Contesting Civilizations of Contemporary India," a review essay (co-authored with Douglas L. Berger) on Gerald James Larson's *India's Agony Over Religion* in *Journal of Dharma* [India] (January-March 2004); "Khizr-i Rah: The Pre-Eminent Guide to Action in Muhammad Iqbal's Thought," *Islamic Studies* [Pakistan] (Spring 2004); "Secular India: Striving Towards a Pluralist Ethos," in *Religions in Dialogue: From Theocracy to Democracy*, ed. Alan Race and Ingrid Shafer (2002); and "The Symbol of Immortality: Some Popular Images of Khidr in the Orient," *Islamic Culture* (July 2000). He is currently working on Islamic perspectives on peace and nonviolence.

Index

Abraham: ancestor of Jesus, 58, 76n3, 82; biblical and Qur'anic stories about, 102; Catholic understanding of, 56-58; compassionate father in Islam, 122; descent from, 70-71; differing understandings of, 116-17; exclusive claims of Jews to, 97-98; and faith in resurrection, 57, 58, 79-80; father of believers, 57-58, 114; father of humanity, 97, 101-5; father of the Jews, 102; focus of interfaith dialogue, 105; founder of true religion, 94; friend of God (*khalil*), 75, 101, 113, 124; *imam*, 74, 86; initiator of the *hajj* pilgrimage, 101, 113; Jews, Christians, and Muslims as children of, 97, 101; model of faith, 56-57, 70, 86, 94, 95, 101, 104, 122; model of hope, 57; model of submission to God's will, 70-71, 74-75, 86, 102, 120; obedience of, 56-57, 86, 120; one who transcends religion, 103-4; prophet, 95, 102; relation with Ishmael, 103, 112; source of blessing for humanity, 86; stock of, 59; and suffering, 74-75; transformation of, in Qur'an, 99-100; true *muslim*, 104

Abrahamic Forum Council, 11-12

Akhenaten: and henotheism, 21, 22, 43, 47

Akiba, Rabbi: and first-century messianism, 50

Al Albait Foundation Colloquia, 9

American Islamic Congress, 5

American Jewish Committee, 5

American Sufi Muslim Association (ASMA): and the Cordoba Initiative, 12; and Jewish–Muslim relations, 5

Anawati, George: and Islam as natural religion, 66

Bar Koziba (Kokhba): and first-century messianism, 50

bilateral relations: Al-Azhar Committee for Dialogue with Monotheistic Religions, 72; International Catholic–Jewish Liaison Committee, 72; International Council of Christians and Jews, 72; Islamic–Catholic Liaison Committee, 72; Pontifical Council for Interreligious Dialogue, 72

bin Talal, El Hassan: and Muslim–Christian dialogue, 3

Carey, George (archbishop of Canterbury): and Muslim–Christian dialogue, 3

Catholic Church: outlook on Islam, 64-72; outlook on Judaism, 58-64; understanding of Abraham, 56-58
celestial origins of Judaism, Christianity, and Islam, 68, 88
Centre d'Études et de Recherches Économiques et Sociales, 3
Christ: as obstacle to Christian–Muslim dialogue, 115; as *ruh allah* in the Qur'an, 124
Christians: appropriation of Hebrew Bible, 87; continuity and discontinuity of, with Jews, 59; and failure of universal Christian faith, 51-52; mission to Jews and Muslims, 63, 92-93; and offensive language toward Jews, 60; and Old Testament, 64-65; as people of the New Covenant, 59, 86
Commission for Religious Relations with Jews (CRRJ), 11, 63
Cordoba Initiative, 12
covenant(s): with Abraham, significance of, 98-99, 112; different interpretations of, 61-63, 86-87, 92; with Israel, 61-63; multi-, and Abrahamic communities, 87; one, with humanity, 87; primordial, 100; with prophets, 100-101; successive, for Christianity, 112-13
Crusades, 36

Declaration on Religious Liberty (*Dignitatis humanae*), 61
Declaration on the Relation of the Catholic Church to Non-Christian Religions (*Nostra Aetate*), 2, 42-43, 58-61, 67-70, 74
Démann, Paul: and Jewish–Christian dialogue, 2
dialogic approach: to interaction among Jews, Christians, and Muslims, 128-30
dialogue: of action, 114; of belief and doctrine, 106-7, 114; bilateral vs. trilateral, 6; and ethical and moral character of society, 135-36; of faith, 107-8, 114-15; and humanization of dialogue partners, 133; interfaith, and Abraham, 104-10; and International Council of Christian and Jews, 2; interreligious, outside the Abrahamic traditions, 15-15n1; interreligious, and self-definition, 60-61, 107; Jewish–Catholic, 2; Jewish–Christian, 1-2; Jewish–Christian, and World Council of Churches, 2; Jewish–Muslim, 4-6, 17n11; of life, 105-6, 114, 124, 136; Muslim–Christian, 2-4; Muslim–Christian, and Catholic Church, 3; Muslim–Christian, and World Council of Churches, 2-3; obstacles to, 107-9; as recognition of the other, 132-36; of religious experience, 115; self-disclosure in, 131-32; and self-knowledge, 131-32; of theological exchange, 114; trilateral, special challenges of, 6-7. *See also* bilateral relations, trialogues, trilateral relations
din: in the Qur'an, 94

earth: as belonging to God alone, in Islam, 96
Elohey Hashshamayim (God[s] of the Heavens), 27

Faruqi, Isma'il al-: role of, in trialogues, 8
Firestone, Reuven: and the Institute for the Study of Jewish–Muslim Interrelations, 5
Fisher, Eugene: on relation of Christians and Jews, 62
Freiburg Circle, 2

Gager, John: and monotheism, 35
Geiger, Abraham: and Judaic influence on Islam, 106-7
God: as absolute and transcendent Truth, 49; of Israel, supremacy of, 27-28; merciful, 29; as one who speaks to humanity, 68-69; reference to, in public life, 74. *See also* monotheism
Gods: conflation of, 25; empire, 26-27; national, 25-26; worshiped by Israel, 23
Groupe de Recherches Islamo-Chrétien, 3
Guidelines for Implementing Nostra Aetate, 60-61

hajj: Abraham as initiator of, 101, 113
hanifs: and monotheism, 22, 38n6, 43; as true *muslim*, 104
Harmatolos, George: and Islam as false religion, 65
Heilbrunn Institute, 5

henotheism: and monotheism, 21
history: Islamic worldview, 96; shared, of Jews, Christians, and Muslims, 126-30
holy war: in ancient Israel and Near East, 25-26, 35-36, 49; Crusades, 36, 49; *jihad*, 36, 49; and monotheism, 35-37
Hugh of Cluny: and Islam as satanic, 65
human beings: as divine and human, 109-10; as stewards of creation, 68

Ibn Khaldun, 'Abd al-Rahman: on theory of world history, 96
imam: meaning of, 74
Institute for the Study of Jewish–Muslim Interrelations, 5
International Council of Christians and Jews (ICCJ), 11
International Scholars' Annual Trialogue (ISAT), 10-11
Interreligious Peace Colloquium (IRPC), 7
Intifada: and Jewish–Muslim relations, 4
Isaacs, Jules: and Jewish–Christian dialogue, 2
Ishmael: legitimacy of, in Qur'an, 98; as prophet, 103; relation with Abraham in Islam, 103; view of Jews on, 97-98, 103; view of Muslims on, 98, 103, 122
Islam: accessible religion, 66; Catholic outlook on, 64-72; false religion, 65; as heresy, 65; monotheistic religion, 43, 67-68;

Islam (*cont.*): natural religion, 66; religion of the Book, 69-70; as satanic, 65
islam: meaning of, 104
Islamic Studies Group (of American Academy of Religion), 8-9
Israel: exclusive monotheism, 43; monotheistic impulse in, 47; military aggression of, and Jewish–Muslim relations, 4
Israel Interfaith Association, 11

Jews: and failure of first-century messianic movement, 50-51; and New Testament, 64-65; offensive language toward, 60
jihad, 36
John Damascene: and Islam as heresy, 65
John Paul II (pope): on common bonds of Christians and Muslims, 71; on the covenant with Israel, 61-63; and Muslim understanding of God, 89
Judaism: Catholic outlook on, 58-64
Justice and Peace Commission (Vatican), 7

Kasper, Walter (cardinal): on mission to Jews, 63-64
Kaufmann, Yehezkel: and triumph of monotheism over polytheism, 47-48
Konrad Adenauer Foundation, 9

Life and Peace Institute, 11
liturgy: Christian, Jewish elements of, 61; link with Abraham and Jewish heritage, 55, 61, 113, 123
Lohfink, Norbert, on theories of covenant, 62
Lumen Gentium: on Muslims, 67
Lutheran World Federation, 11

Maimonides Foundation, 5
Massignon, Louis: and Islam as Abrahamic religion, 66
Middle East: conflict in, and trialogues, 15
mission: aggressive activity of, 121; of Christians, to Jews and Muslims, 63-64, 92-93
monotheism: among ancient Israelites, 21-22; emergence of, 21-24, 42-45; exclusive, 29-30, 43; extremely exclusive, 34; expression of divine essence, 53; Greco-Roman interest in, 33; Hellenistic expressions of, 22; and *hanifs*, 22; inclusive, 25, 28, 29; innate in human beings, 43; and inter-monotheistic polemic, 34-35; and Jewish–Christian competition, 35, 44; in polytheistic world, 32; priority over polytheism, 47; and quest for Supreme Being, 47; and the threat of Roman polytheism, 35; and Ugarit, 22; unifying system, 20
monotheisms: competition among, 30-31, 33-34; different anthropologies and theologies among, 37; early, 32-33; plural usage, 44-45

Muhammad: obstacle to Christian–Muslim dialogue, 115; prophet, 69, 83, 88
multilateral dialogue: Temple of Understanding, 73; United Religions Initiative, 73; World Conference of Religions for Peace, 73
Muslim–Jewish–Christian Conference (MJCC), 7-8
Muslims: and failure to compete with Western and non-Western nations, 52-53; and human beings as stewards of creation, 68; importance of faith for, 69; and Old Testament, 64-65; as unbelievers, 65-66; Vatican II on, 66-71

new religious movements (NRM), 30-31; nonapplicability of, to Christianity and Islam, 44; in polytheistic environment, 31-32; and vocabulary of market economy, 31, 49
New Testament: divine origin of, as Protestant idea, 87, 93

Office of Interreligious Relations (of WCC), 11

patrilineal vs. matrilineal descent, 98
Paul VI (pope): on brotherhood of Christians and Muslims, 71-72
peace and justice: Jewish, Christian, and Muslim collaboration for, 136-38
People of the Book, 69-70

pluralism, religious: in the Qur'an, 109
polytheism: biblical memories of, 22-23; decline of, 24-26; international worldview of, 26; priority of monotheism to, 47; as threat to monotheism, 32
Pontifical Council for Interreligious Dialogue, 3, 16nn6, 7; 11
prophets, in Islam, 95-96

Qur'an: and mystery of Christ, 93

religions: celestial 68, 88; idolatrous, 88
revelation: in Catholic teaching, 91; of God, in scriptures of Jews, Muslims, and Christians, 81, 117; views of, as obstacles to dialogue, 108-9
Royal Academy for Islamic Civilization, 3

salvation: history, centered on Christ for Christians, 92; prefigured in the exodus, 82
Schmidt, Wilhelm: and priority of monotheism over polytheism, 47
scripture(s): Catholic understanding of, 93; competing, in Abrahamic religions, 80-81; dialogue with other traditions', 118-19, 121-22, 134; human role in composition of, 117-18, 119n1, 121-22; as living text, 91-92, 93; revelation of God in, 81, 117
shahada: as ultimate statement of Islamic faith, 83

Sharbil, Mar: as model for rise of Israelite monotheism, 48
shirk, and true faith in God, 74, 87n22
social action: of Jews and Christians, 61
Spanish Association of Muslim–Christian Friendship, 3
Stark, Rodney: and emergence of new religious movements (NRM), 30-31, 49

Thomas Aquinas: and Muslims as unbelievers, 65-66
Thompson, Thomas: and emerging monotheism, 24-30
Three Faiths Forum, 12
Trialogue of the Abrahamic Faiths, 9-10
trialogues (Jewish–Christian–Muslim): and clarification of beliefs and practices, 13-14; and collaboration among Jews, Christians, and Muslims, 15; conferences, 19n33; and Middle East conflict, 11, 15; topics of, 13-15. *See also* trilateral relations
trilateral relations: Les Enfants d'Abraham, 73; Fraternité d'Abraham, 73; Three Faiths Forum, 73
Trinity, rejected by Muslims, 88, 134
truth: possibility of, in other traditions, 81, 117, 133-34

William, Rowan (archbishop of Canterbury): and Muslim–Christian dialogue, 3
witness: of Christians toward Jews, 60, 63-64
word, divine: in Jewish, Muslim, and Christian scriptures, 109
World Conference on Religion and Peace (Japanese chapter), 11
World Islamic Call Society, 3

YHWH, and Egyptian theism, 47

www.ingramcontent.com/pod-product-compliance
Lightning Source LLC
Chambersburg PA
CBHW051104160426
43193CB00010B/1308